THE SPIRITUAL PATH
OF
CARYLL HOUSELANDER

THE SPIRITUAL PATH
OF
CARYLL HOUSELANDER

Joyce Kemp

PAULIST PRESS
New York/Mahwah, N.J.

Acknowledgments—
Grateful acknowledgement is made for permission to use excerpts from:
The Christian Community Bible. Copyright © 1988 by Bernardo Hurault.
Reprinted by permission of Claretian Publications, Quezon City, Philippines. *The
Search for the Beloved* by Jean Houston. Copyright © 1987 by Jean Houston.
Reprinted by permission of the author. *Public Like a Frog,* by Jean Houston. Copy-
right © 1993 by Jean Houston. Reprinted by permission of the author. *Caryll
Houselander, That Divine Eccentric* by Maisie Ward. Copyright © 1962 by Maisie
Ward. Reprinted by permission of Wilfrid Sheed. *The Letters of Caryll Houselander
and Her Spiritual Legacy,* edited by Maisie Ward. Copyright © 1965 by Maisie
Ward. Reprinted by permission of Wilfrid Sheed. *The Splendor of the Rosary, with
Prayers by Caryll Houselander* by Maisie Ward. Copyright © 1945 by Maisie Ward.
Reprinted by permission of Wilfrid Sheed. Every effort has been made to identify
sources for all quoted material. In the event acknowledgments were omitted, we will
make corrections or additions in subsequent editions.

Cover design by Cheryl Finbow

Library of Congress Cataloging-in-Publication Data

Kemp, Joyce.
    The spiritual path of Caryll Houselander / Joyce Kemp.
        p. cm. — (Jung and spirituality)
    Includes bibliographical references.
    ISBN 0-8091-4006-3
    1. Houselander, Caryll. 2. Art therapists—England—Biography. 3. Spiritual
life—Catholic Church. I. Title. II. Series.

BX4705.H758 K45 2000
282'.092—dc21
[B]

00-047887

Published by Paulist Press
997 Macarthur Boulevard
Mahwah, New Jersey 07430

www.paulistpress.com

Printed and bound in the
United States of America

Contents

SERIES FOREWORD

The Jung and Spirituality series provides a forum for the critical interaction between Jungian psychology and living spiritual traditions. The series serves two important goals.

The first goal is: *To enhance a creative exploration of the contributions and criticisms that Jung's psychology can offer to religion.* Jungian thought has far-reaching implications for the understanding and practice of spirituality. Interest in these implications continues to expand in both Christian and non-Christian religious communities. People are increasingly aware of the depth and insight that a Jungian perspective adds to the human experiences of the sacred. And yet, the use of Jungian psychoanalysis clearly does not eliminate the need for careful philosophical, theological, and ethical reflection or for maintaining one's centeredness in a spiritual tradition.

The second goal is: *To bring the creative insights and critical tools of religious studies and practice to bear on Jungian thought.* Many volumes in the Jung and Spirituality series work to define the borders of the Jungian and spiritual traditions, to bring the spiritual dimensions of Jung's work into relief, and to deepen those dimensions. We believe that an important outcome of the Jung-Spirituality dialogue is greater cooperation of psychology and spirituality. Such cooperation will move us ahead in the formation of a postmodern spirituality, equal to the challenges of the twenty-first century.

Robert L. Moore
Series Editor

In loving memory of my parents,
Arthur and Tillie Kemp,

and for all whose support made this
book possible.
You know who you are.

Introduction

"I came to cast fire upon the earth, and would that it were already kindled," Jesus says in the Gospel of St. Luke (12:49). Caryll Houselander, with her fiery red hair, passion for life, and ability to carve unforgettable images of God with words, might have said the same thing. She was a laywoman ahead of her time—an artist, poet, social activist and mystic who found God in everything. Her words, written in the 1940s and 1950s, speak clearly to the issues of our day: a lack of creative imagination, an other-worldly spirituality that discounts what is human and earthy, mental illness, homelessness, the marginalization of millions of people through prejudice and oppression, and the atrocities of war. She criticized the human tendency to give way to hatred and to seek vengeance, especially on an international level. Such a view, she pointed out, is contrary to the teachings of Christ, who commanded us to love our enemies and to be good to those who hate us.

Caryll's spirituality is for everyone, not just monks and nuns. It is for people who have no time to pray in peace and quiet. She knew that we can be as holy washing the dishes, changing diapers, cleaning the house, sweeping the street or working in an office as we are kneeling in church with our hands folded in prayer. She

1

created a form of contemplation in daily life for herself called *rhythms* to deal with the lack of solitude and peaceful atmosphere necessary for prayer in her life. When she shared her idea of rhythms with others, they, too, found some inner peace for their souls in the midst of the noise and distractions of their environment.

Caryll was one of the first expressive arts therapists, bringing about the healing of "incurable" patients sent to her by a London psychiatrist in an era when art and music were not accepted as a therapeutic tool. She founded an organization called The Loaves and Fishes to give aid discreetly to people who fell through the cracks of the welfare system.

Caryll's greatest gift to us today, however, is her understanding that each one of us is called to be Christ in the world. Each of us is to live out, in a unique way, some aspect of the Christ-life. We are to cast fire, to spread love, by giving Christ to each other as simply as he gives himself to us in sacramental form. We bring Christ to others through words and kindness, through work and friendship, and through the ability to comfort one another. Her spirituality is biblically based and echoes Paul's writings on the Mystical Body of Christ in his letters to the Corinthians and the Ephesians. Her words make dry doctrine come alive. The images she creates touch our deepest emotions. Her spirituality is incarnated. She does not dichotomize body and soul, nor does she picture the body as the source of all evil. Caryll points out that although humans are capable of smearing everything they touch, they also leave touches of beauty wherever they go.[1]

It is through the body that we experience joy, beauty, wonder and gratitude as well as pain and suffering.

The psychology of Carl Jung also shines forth in Caryll's writings, especially her love of myth and symbol and her belief that the great repression of our age is not the repression of sex, but the repression of Christ in us.[2]

The Christ-seed in many of us lies dormant. In order to bring it to life, we must die to ourselves, like seeds in the earth dying to give birth to the plant. Caryll saw that even during times when the soul seems to be shut down and a winter of the spirit makes it almost impossible to pray, Christ is growing toward the spring of his flowering in us.

Caryll's life is presented here as a work of art that is complete. By studying her life experience and her spiritual journey, we can find wisdom and guidance for our own. Transformation and healing happen when we place our individual life experience in the context of a larger story. The principles underlying this approach are based upon the works of three people: Dr. Ira Progoff (1921–1998), St. Ignatius of Loyola (1491–1556) and Dr. Jean Houston (1939–). All three bring together the spiritual life and holistic depth psychology, providing methods for becoming both more human and more contemplative.

Ira Progoff speaks of dynamic processes at work in the depths of the human psyche as means that enable the goals, the interior strivings that emerge out of our "naked being" to be brought to fulfillment.[3]

He uses the term "seed potential" to describe what lies within us. His Life-Study approach to the Intensive Journal® method enables one to enter into the life of a person whose time on earth has come to completion. By keeping a journal as this person, we are able to enhance

3

our own awareness of the rhythms and cycles of life. We enter into processes that bring about both creative expression and personal integration.

St. Ignatius of Loyola invites us to meditate upon our ability to choose, to say yes or no to Christ's invitation to follow him. His *Spiritual Exercises* have been used for more than 400 years to deepen one's relationship with the Divine through the use of active imagination in prayer. St. Ignatius handed down a method to discern God's action and call in our lives through attention to inner events and movements as we meditate upon and contemplate the life of Christ. This process allows the life of divine grace to grow in us, the same life that was realized in the birth, death and resurrection of Jesus Christ, who embodies the fulfillment of all human searching and longing for union with the infinite.[4]

Jean Houston describes her practice of sacred psychology as a transformational journey beyond our little "local selves" to the full flowering of the "Godseed" within us and a sharing in the Christic pattern of birth, death and resurrection to new life.[5]

She challenges us to become full participants in and cocreators of the historical, the mythic, and the unitive realms of experience. She refers to these three realms as THIS IS ME, WE ARE and I AM. They encompass the movement from everyday, ordinary existence through the realms of the symbolic to that of the presence of God.

Caryll Houselander simply states that each of us is another Christ. In some he lies dead in the tomb, like an ancient seed lying fallow in the grave of an Egyptian pharaoh. In others he is a caricature mirroring the idols we have created on the altars of our egoism and worship of false gods. Caryll believed that as our conception of Christ becomes more true, our minds grow broader and deeper; our hearts become warmer, wiser, and kinder; our humor is more tender; our senses are more alive; our compassion is stronger; our capacity for giving and receiving increases. We become radiant, for the light of Christ flames within us.[6]

This book is an attempt to combine a narrative biography of the life of Caryll Houselander, an overview of her spirituality and spiritual exercises. The purpose of the exercises is to help those engaged in them to see in Caryll's story something of their own life history. By looking at Caryll's life and her understanding of the spiritual life, they will find parallels in theirs. Suggestions are provided for groups and for individuals.

Chapter 1 invites you to look at the birth and early childhood of Caryll Houselander and the circumstances into which she was born. There are many factors in our lives that are givens: our family, the time in history during which we live, our country and ethnic group, our race, our sex, certain genetic dispositions. All have an impact upon us. We are also born with the potential to become the unique person we were meant to be. The Book of Genesis says that human beings were created in the image and likeness of God. One of the divine aspects we share as humans is the ability to create. As far as we know, we are the only species with the capacity to rise above the basic conditions and events of our lives. An acorn becomes an oak tree, a tadpole becomes a frog. The human fetus is not nearly as limited in its unfolding. Through the story of the life of Caryll Houselander we will discover the many factors involved in the development of our own potential: physical, mental, emotional and spiritual.

Chapters 2 and 3 address the wounding that comes into each of our lives, all the ways we are sinned against. That life is difficult does not excuse us from accepting responsibility for our behavior, especially as adults. Our very wounds can become the source of our strength and the inspiration for our work in the world. Jean Houston, in an excellent chapter on "The Sacred Wound,"[7] points out that wounds become sacred when we are willing to stay open to the pain and allow the engagement of the Great Story. When we let go of our old story with all its scabs and scars, a new redemptive story can manifest itself in and through us. The loss of trust that comes with the experience of betrayal can be overcome in a similar manner. In a Christian context, we might enter into the larger story of the betrayals of Jesus by Judas and by Peter in our imagination and cry out with Jesus on the Cross, "Father, forgive them; they do not know what they are doing" (Luke 23:34).

Chapter 4 tells the story of Caryll's relationship with a family friend called Smoky. He had a significant impact on her life and education. Smoky was a mentor and a confidant, one who was able to call her to account with tough love at times. He used play to teach Caryll and her sister Ruth many things about the world and about history. The exercises at the end of this chapter are based upon free play, a kind of play that is creative and noncompetitive. Free play taps into the genius of the child within each of us.

Chapters 5, 6 and 7 deal with Caryll's search for a true spiritual home, one that resonated with her own mystical experiences. Throughout her life, she struggled to be sure that what she said and wrote were in tune with orthodox theology. She left the Roman Catholic Church in a fit of anger when an usher was more concerned about her pew rent than her soul. She explored many religions but ultimately returned to the Roman Catholic Church, not because she agreed with all of its practices, but because her visions led her to believe it was where she belonged. Each of us needs to go through a period of questioning if we are to make the faith of our childhood our own and not just a set of tenets we accept because someone else said they were true. The exercises are designed to help you explore your own inner experiences and beliefs and to discover what is true for you.

Chapters 8 and 9 deal with Caryll as a social artist. The experience of living during two World Wars had an indelible impact upon her. She contemplated the passion of Christ in the suffering that war imposed upon all involved. She wrote to a friend that before the war she used to rage at the worldliness of so-called Christianity. Even though this kind of Christianity continued to exist, she said it wasn't real. True Christianity, according to Caryll, does not depend upon what school of thought we grew up in or what creed we believe, but on our capacity for love and for humility. Caryll's idea of humility was influenced by her love for the Russian Orthodox image of Christ, humble, suffering and crowned with thorns. True Christianity, in her mind, is found in simple people and in those who nurture the inner life of the spirit.[8]

Caryll would have adopted today's "option for the poor" passionately. She seemed to be drawn to the down and out, the homeless, the marginalized. Her compassion for those who fell through the cracks of the welfare system, for prostitutes and for those who were in mental hospitals, was not a condescending handout. She identified with the people who were suffering, genuinely acting as if she were no better than they were. The exercises invite you to reflect upon how the passion of Christ continues in the world today and how you might be called to minister to the suffering Christ in others.

The final three chapters explore Caryll's spiritual legacy. The exercises in them invite you to enter into her spirit and to become a member of her Wisdom School.

SUGGESTIONS FOR WORKING WITH THIS BOOK

Groups who choose to journey together need to meet regularly and make a commitment to attend every session. You may prefer to do the exercises during a long weekend. Participants would either have to read the text ahead of time or designate a leader to tell the story of Caryll's life before engaging in the exercises. Dialogue about the aspects of her life in each chapter that resonate with those of the participants helps to deepen the correlation between the patterns of individual lives and the larger pattern that Caryll's life represents. Each group needs a Guide. The Guide needs to be thoroughly familiar with the material and have some understanding of group process. The Guide needs to be sensitive to what is happening in the group without being controlling, trying to play therapist or preaching. You may prefer to take turns as the Guide. Materials, resources and timing are listed at the beginning of each exercise. Time frames are approximations and may vary according to the size of the group and other factors. Some time needs to be provided after each experience to process what has happened. Simple questions such as "How do you feel right now?" or "What did you learn from this exercise?" can help participants to reflect upon their experience.

You who are working alone with this text need to record the Scripts for the Guide on an audiocassette and then listen to them as you enter into the exercise. You may want to find a companion to help you process your experiences.

> May God bless you on your journey.
> The measured beat of Love,
> with pure perfection of music,
> timing the life of Christ
> in the human heart
> goes on.[9]

Chapter 1:
Beginnings

Indeed if we could open the book of everyone's childhood, we should know the story of their lives so far as essential things are concerned without anything else.[1]

Caryll Houselander believed that our whole life lies hidden in our childhood, like the life of a flower or a tree in the seed. She knew that what is hidden cannot always be brought into the light, especially in early childhood. Sometimes it remains buried for decades, covered by layers and layers of personal choices and external circumstances. This was true of Caryll herself. Extremely sensitive to the beauty around her and gifted with the ability to describe her experiences in verse, she was at heart a poet. Her keen insight into the souls of those who came to her for guidance reveals psychic abilities as well. Her highly developed inner life reflects that of a mystic.

Caryll was born in the city of Bath at the turn of the century, October 29, 1901, and was named after a boat on which her mother, Gertrude Provis, had spent a great deal of time during her pregnancy. Caryll's life was fragile from the beginning. Her uncle, Francis Provis, a gynecologist, said she looked like a tiny red fish at birth.

He called a clergyman to baptize her immediately, since he didn't think she would survive. He joked that either she would drown in the baptismal waters because she was so small and odd, or she would swim away in them like the fish she resembled. The clergyman stormed out of the house when her parents, unable to decide upon a name for her, started arguing and laughing. So Francis baptized her himself, calling her Frances Caryll. The joke on all of them was that she took a turn for the better and survived.

The times in which Caryll lived were turbulent. Caryll's birth occurred ten months after the death of Queen Victoria. As ruler of England for sixty-three years, the queen had been the only source of stability in an era of many changes. During her reign the country's population doubled. New wealth had begun to invade England's old exclusive society. World Fairs celebrated a growing global economy, and the principle of progress fed a growing materialism. Caryll witnessed the growth of new towns, institutions, social classes and nations. New movements made themselves felt. Writers such as William Butler Yeats, T. S. Eliot, James Joyce, Virginia Woolf, George Bernard Shaw and James Matthew Barrie represented the trends in literature and drama. Darwin and others expounded on the theory of evolution and the survival of the fittest. Caryll reflected upon these developments when she wrote:

> There is a young man who lives
> in the world of progress.
> He used to worship a God
> Who was kind to him.
> The God had a long, white beard.

He lived in the clouds.
But, all the same,
He was close to the solemn child
who had secretly
shut Him up in a picture book.
But now
the man is enlightened.
Now he has been to school
and has learned to kick a ball
and to be abject
in the face of public opinion.
He knows, too,
that men are hardly removed from monkeys.
You see, he lives in the light
of the twentieth century.[2]

On a political level, socialism was growing. In 1906, the Liberals took over Parliament. In 1911 they managed to pass an act to pay salaries to members of the House of Commons so that poor unionists could afford to seek office. In 1912 Parliament passed the National Health Insurance Act and unemployment benefits. The beginning of Irish Home Rule during the same year ignited conflict in heavily Protestant Ulster that has yet to be resolved completely. Karl Marx wrote the *Communist Manifesto,* and the Russian revolution adopted its principles.

Catholicism had grown in England due to the birth of a revival movement, but Catholics were still identified with the working class. During the first decade of the twentieth century, religion in general took an increasingly defensive stance as people responded more and more to science and the growth of depth psychology.

Caryll was affected both by a renewed enthusiasm for Roman Catholicism and by the prejudice among the English against it. Although her parents identified themselves as Protestants, they had practiced no religion at all. Then, due to the influence of two friends, Gertrude decided to have her girls baptized Roman Catholic when Caryll was six years old. This explains why Caryll later referred to herself as a "rocking-horse Catholic," one who was not born into the faith.

After she was baptized, Caryll received little religious instruction. Caryll learned about God during the first years of her life from her nurse, Rose Francis, who taught her to say grace after meals. It seemed to her, however, that Rose Francis' real religion was good manners, based upon what little ladies did and didn't do. They did not stir their porridge or blow on it. They did not drink from their saucer, swing on the garden gate or speak to the postman. The latter, Caryll realized later in life, was because her nurse hoped to speak to the postman herself, a man whom she eventually married. The cook showed Caryll pictures of God appearing through blue gaps of sky in the clouds. He wore a white robe and a kind of red scarf and looked just liked her father's former groom, Bill Reynolds. Bill had long white hair that grew down to his shoulders and a long white beard that grew very nearly down to his waist. He had blue eyes like periwinkles, apple cheeks, a cherry nose and a thunderous laugh. He seemed to be the most ancient man in the world to Caryll. His coat was so old that it had taken the shape of his magnificent, broad-shouldered body. Similar images of coats worn to the shape of one's body appear often in her books.

Caryll's father Wilmott came from a large family who lived in a fine house, Wick Court, near Bristol. He was always full of jokes and used strong language. He claimed to be descended from a Dutch pirate who ended his life hung in chains on an English dock. Caryll's parents met on a hunting field. Wilmott was a fine horseman. Gertrude preferred the tennis court and traveling abroad. A friend described Caryll's mother as a horsey, sporting type with fair hair, a fine figure and blue eyes that looked one through and through. She seems to have had a sense of humor not unlike her husband's. One Christmas she joined her friend Marguerite Fedden for Midnight Mass. Intrigued by the confessional, she peeped in, laughing quietly and making jokes. Obviously, this was before her own conversion.

Caryll's sister Ruth was two years older than she was. In her autobiography, *A Rocking-Horse Catholic,* Caryll notes that she did not remember being aware of her sister until the age of two. At that time, her sister was sent to a nursing home in Margate to be treated for tuberculosis. When Caryll went to visit her, Ruth's hair had been cropped like a boy's and she was painfully thin. Caryll recalled that her sister did not seem happy to see her, perhaps because she regretted leaving her playmates. A matron referred to Ruth as the "little zebra." When she returned home, Caryll told everyone "I have a sister; she is a zebra." Caryll suffered acutely when they laughed because she did not understand the humor in what she had said.

From infancy, Caryll was alive to beauty—the sound of melodious church bells, the view of the hills that encircled the city of Bath, the vibrant colors of her father's rose garden, the fluff of canary hair on the head of the niece of her nurse. Before she was old enough to write, Caryll would compose poems and ask an adult, usually her father, to write them down. Her earliest one, an ethical commentary, read:

> Let's all be a jolly lot.
> Let no one be forgot.
> We can't be a jolly lot
> If anyone is forgot.

One of Caryll's most vivid memories from early childhood was that of her father's rose garden. It was a long way from their house, perched on a hill and surrounded by high gray stone walls. Caryll came into it through a low and narrow wooden door. Inside, several banks covered in ferns converged into miniature green valleys. They seemed magical, ideal for child's play. The garden was filled with roses, even ones that created a roof above Caryll's head. Through them she could see tiny patches of blue sky, glimpsed between shades of red, gold, white, cream, orange and pink. Years later, Caryll imagined that one must enter the kingdom of heaven through a door not unlike that of her father's garden, one just high enough for a child. In her mind, an adult would have to enter bowed low or on one's knees through a very low, narrow door made from the wood of the Cross.

All children go through a stage where they are afraid of monsters under the bed or bogeymen chasing them up and down the stairs. Caryll tells how she imagined the worst bogey living in an enormous drainpipe that she passed by on a daily walk with one of the servants, who told her that the huge yawning hole on the side of the road was the home of "Mr. Tayler." Caryll passed Mr. Tayler's lair in fear and trembling, especially if she had been naughty, for his hunger and his ferocity were insatiable. She never told anyone about her fears. Had she done so, she reflected later, they would have laughed Mr. Tayler to scorn, and possibly laughed him out of her consciousness.

When Caryll was three, the cook who banged the pots and sang hymns about heaven all day slit her own throat in an attempt to reach the promised land. Then Caryll's family moved to Brighton, where another cook prowled around the house at night stealing things like bits of toothpaste. Caryll watched at night under half-closed eyelids. The governess, Miss Flynn, liked to roam the house at night dressed as a witch. She would enter Caryll's room, sit on her bed, and fix her with a penetrating stare full of malign amusement. These terrors left their mark, as Caryll was unusually sensitive to emotional currents and sensory experience.

Caryll lived through two world wars. They left an indelible mark upon her. She compared the experience of war to the passion of Christ. In fact, one of her first books was entitled *This War Is the Passion*. Caryll was able to see that human suffering is bearable only to the degree that we are one with Christ. Our identification with Christ, especially with him in his passion, gives us the strength to bear the suffering of the world.

> For nine months Christ grew in His Mother's body. Working, eating, sleeping she was forming His body from hers. His flesh and blood. From her humanity she gave him his humanity.[3]

Exercise 1.1 Loosening the Soil of Our Life

Materials needed: *Paper and pencil.*
Approximate time: *One hour.*
Script for Guide: We can see in the stories of Caryll's childhood hints of what she would become. As soil is to the seed, the years of infancy and early childhood provided the foundation for the rest of her life. All of us are born coded to unfold into a fully human being, just as the acorn becomes the oak and the egg becomes the chicken. Yet, unlike plants and animals, each of us has a greater range of possibilities. The circumstances into which we are born, as well as our genetic coding, color our development. If we look back, we see that early patterns have continued to repeat themselves throughout our life with greater and greater complexity. Due to circumstances, some of our potential still may lie dormant, waiting to be planted, nurtured and allowed to flower.

Take some time now to look at the soil of your life and the hidden seeds of your own becoming. Recall as many memories as you can of the earliest years of your life, from your birth until the age of four or five. Since many are held in your body and are not verbal, you may want to draw images rather than paint pictures in words. Look at the way you were cultivated by the society, the family structure, the ethnic traditions and the period of history into which you were born.

When were you born? Where? Into what level of society were you born? What religion, if any, did your parents or caretakers practice? Describe your parents and siblings. What role did grandparents play in your early life? Aunts and uncles? Cousins? What were some of your family traditions? What other significant adults helped to form and nurture you?

What personality traits were apparent in you practically from birth? What characteristics typical of your parents do you see in yourself? What image would you use to symbolize the emotional tone and general atmosphere of your early childhood?

Tell the story of your physical life. What was the state of your health? How did you feel about your body and your physical appearance? What games did you like to play? How did you get along with others, especially playmates? What were your favorite pastimes? Was there anything that impeded your growth physically, emotionally or spiritually?

Early childhood is the period in our life when we learn to trust others. Caryll's parents did not seem to be there for her most of the time. She may have learned trust through experiences with servants and caretakers such as her nurse, Rose Francis. Servants like her governess may have led her to be overly cautious. What aspects of Caryll's early childhood resonate with your own? How has the development of trust or lack of it manifested itself in your life?

Group process: *Share your reflections with another person and then process your experience in pairs with the rest of the group.*

For those working alone: *Reread your reflections aloud. What additional memories, feelings and perceptions do you experience as you read? Do you see any seeds of what you have become in your childhood?*

Record what comes to you as you reread as an additional entry in your journal.

Exercise 1.2 Sensory Awareness

Caryll was alive to the world around her from an early age. She drew upon all of her senses to create poetic images:

- the hard bark of a tree
- the touch of delicate grass
- the warmth of the sun
- the murmuring voice of the sea
- the blight on a green leaf
- the smells of linen, lemon oil and soap in a boarding school
- the taste of bananas reserved for special feasts

We have dulled our senses. We have tuned out the noise of street traffic and the hum of the refrigerator. We do not see the homeless in the city and the plastic bags caught in barren tree branches. We block out the smells from landfills and the exhaust of diesel trucks. We fear being touched. We dull aching muscles with painkillers. In an attempt to block out the unpleasant, we have also deprived ourselves of much of life's beauty, including the presence of God. We must recapture the ability to see, hear, feel, taste and smell with all the awe and wonder of a child.

A. *Opening the Doors of Sensory Perception*

Materials needed: *A place to walk outside or, if you prefer to stay indoors, a variety of foods, aromatic oils, or objects—hot, cold, hard, soft, rough, smooth, etc.*

Approximate time: *Thirty minutes.*

Script for Guide. One simple exercise to enhance sensory awareness is to take thirty-minute walks. Limit each walk to one of the senses. For example, you could begin by concentrating on vision. As you walk, look at what is around you as though you had been blind for many years and were seeing everything for the first time. Notice colors, shapes, movement. On another walk, pay attention to odors—the fragrance of flowers in the neighbor's garden, the smell of bread baking at the corner deli, the foul, musty stench of the city sewer, the pungent fragrance of the newly mown alfalfa field. On a third, listen to the sounds around you—the songs of birds, the hum of an airplane overhead, the laughter of children playing in a schoolyard.

Instead of taking a walk, you may want to have a smorgasbord of tastes—foods that are salty, sweet, bitter, bland, juicy, dry, soft, rubbery, crunchy or slippery. Test your sense of smell with a wide spectrum of fragrances, or experiment with the sense of touch by feeling various fabrics, woods, metals, stones and plants. Try feeling objects with your eyes closed and notice the difference when you are unable to see.

B. Finding an Object

Materials needed: *A bowl of leaves from the same bush or tree or a bowl of one kind of fruit.*

Approximate time: *Fifteen minutes.*

Script for Guide: A game that can be both fun and enlightening is picking a piece of fruit or a leaf from a group in a basket. Use only one kind of fruit or leaf in the pile. Study your leaf or piece of fruit carefully. Look at it, smell it, feel it. When you think you know it well, return the object to the basket and mix it in among the rest. Then see if you can find yours again. You will discover, much to your amazement, that it is quite easy to find your piece of fruit or leaf, for each one is unique, even though superficially all may appear to be similar.

Group process: *After each exercise, take at least ten minutes to reflect upon and record what happened to you. Pay particular attention to inner movements—confusion and clarity, resistance and attraction, positive and negative feelings. Over time, you will begin to see patterns that reveal a thread of continuity running through the unfolding of your life. Those who wish may share what they have learned about themselves with the group.*

For those working alone: *Write about your experiences after each exercise, noting inner movements in particular: confusion and clarity, resistance and attraction, positive and negative feelings. Do not judge one as better than the other. Begin to look for patterns in these movements. You may see a thread of continuity emerging. Record what you notice when you reread what you have written.*

Prayer

> Let us too become as little children,
> to find the Divine Child
> in our own hearts.[4]

Chapter 2:
Sacred Wounding

...our wounds are solitary stars
answering out of the night
to the Light of God.[1]

Sometime between the ages of five and six, Caryll moved with her family to Brighton. Not long afterward, she and her sister, who had returned from Margate, were baptized in the Catholic Church of the Sacred Heart. A friend, George Spencer Bower, convinced their mother that if one was going to be Christian at all, one might as well be Roman Catholic. In spite of his belief, he could not bring himself to embrace Catholicism because of its teachings on the virginity of Mary. Bower was a lawyer and an agnostic, known to the children simply as "Smoky." Caryll described him as the most lovable person she ever knew. Caryll was not interested in religion and detested the "little altars" her suddenly pious mother insisted the girls build in their bedrooms, mostly because she had to spend the bulk of her pocket money on flowers, vases, statues, lamps, candles, candlesticks, lace and linen altar cloths.

Not long before her first communion and confession several years later, two things happened that brought about a complete change in her inner life. The first was the sudden exit of her beloved governess, Rose Francis, which left Caryll grieved and empty. The second was the departure of her mother for an extended tour of Spain. Her sister Ruth was sent to board in a local convent, but Caryll was kept at home to do exactly as she pleased while her father was at work. Supplied with ample money, she wandered around Bristol where they were living. She spent time reading in bookstores and sat for hours in church, a place where she felt less alone.

One day, as she stepped into the church, Caryll happened upon a Redemptorist mission, a series of talks calling for repentance and the mending of one's ways. In those days, the presentations were filled with threats of hellfire and damnation. The preacher was a gigantic man with snowy white hair and a face like an eagle. She watched him walk down the aisle with a deliberate, heavy slowness. His footsteps reminded her of pallbearers, and the loudness of their measured tread suggested to her the approach of doom. In her autobiography she pictured him ascending the pulpit slowly, pausing for what seemed an interminable time, and leaning over the congregation in his flowing black robes, one large black crucifix in his belt, another and bigger one behind him. He spread his arms like an eagle's wings while his eyes traveled slowly around the church, searching each face in turn, as if he could penetrate through the pious masks that concealed the awful state of the sinners' souls. When the tension was at its height and they were all holding their breath, he said, "Perhaps there is someone in this church tonight who is in mortal sin—someone whose soul is *dead*."[2] Several innocent ladies exchanged uneasy, suspicious glances and one or two young men reddened in the gathering dusk. Then the preacher drew a vivid word picture of a person in mortal sin. He spared no details in his picture of a person shut up in a dark room with a decomposing corpse. As this person fumbled in the dark, the awful body was discovered. A tiny chink of gray light filtering into the room through a crack rested upon the appalling sight.

After the sermon, Caryll walked home through the dark streets trembling. When her mother returned from Spain the next day laden with gifts, Caryll begged her to make arrangements for her first confession. Her mother told Caryll to speak about it herself to the priest giving the mission. He turned out to be a gentle and kind man. He promised to hear her confession at the end of the mission and to allow her to receive communion the following day. She made her confession on the tenth of March, but before she could receive her first communion, she fell violently ill with a chill that developed into a long illness. She finally made her first communion in July on the Feast of the Precious Blood. There were no special white dresses, candles or flowers. She went to the altar dressed just like anyone else on an ordinary day.

No doubt the remnants of the trauma of the mission sermon led to a sudden illness that prevented her from going to communion a second time. She was walking upstairs, somewhat unwillingly, to wash her hands for tea when, without a moment's warning, she became too weak to take another step. She sat down on a stair feeling as if all of her life was flowing out of her heels. Her wrists were too weak to lift her hands. The servants carried her to her room where she remained bedridden for

25

three months. She had difficulty breathing, had a continual fever and grew weaker by the day. Tormented with feelings of guilt, she insisted on confiding her sins to her mother almost daily. By this time her mother had become Catholic herself and was devoted to a priest who paid daily visits to their house. Each afternoon he spent hours listening to Caryll's confessions. They were filled with grossly exaggerated transgressions, many sheer inventions. Nothing helped. Finally she asked to receive communion. She had an inner sense that if she did, she would be healed. But her doctor refused her request, believing it would snap her last thread of sanity. He also wisely forbade her to make any more confessions, relenting only when she was near death. The priest came in the evening to give her *viaticum,* a piece of a consecrated host intended to help the soul on its way to God. Flames of firelight danced on the walls of her darkened room, causing pain like scalding water falling on an open wound whenever she opened her eyes. Now she no longer attempted to translate her torment as the punishment of particular sins. She realized in a dim, intuitive way that it was not anything she had *done* that required forgiveness, but everything that she *was* that needed to be miraculously transformed. "It was of *myself* that I required to be healed, and that could only happen one way, by a union in which I would be quite lost in God, and *that* I knew could only happen in Holy Communion."[3]

Caryll, as young as she was, had an inner wisdom that told her how her healing would take place. She had learned from experience that confessing imaginary sins did not relieve her anxiety. She was suffering from excessive feelings of guilt that had no apparent cause. The cure for this case of scruples was union with God and the experience of unconditional love. She recalled experiencing an instant sense of peace the minute the wafer was placed on her tongue, as if she had awakened from a long nightmare to the security and blessedness of a sunlit morning. The lights that previously had caused such pain now shone through her thin eyelids and suffused her whole being. She sat up and demanded that her little toy soldiers be brought to her on a tray. The priest ordered her to lie down and say her communion thanksgiving prayers, but she refused. When her soldiers were brought to her and put on the altar at her bedside, she fell peacefully asleep.

After this experience, it was impossible for Caryll to doubt the presence of Christ in the sacrament of holy communion or its preservation in the Catholic Church, no matter how good or bad, wise or foolish its hierarchy, priests and members might be. Just as Catherine of Siena, a saint whom Caryll admired, believed the Catholic Church was God's in spite of its earthly corruption, so did she. This belief did not prevent her from leaving the church in a fit of anger as a young adult, but ultimately it brought her back in spite of how she felt.

The only person other than Caryll who believed she had been miraculously cured was Smoky. He arrived from London the next day saying, "It takes an old agnostic like me to believe in God!" The doctors declared that there hadn't been anything wrong with her in the first place, nothing worse than hysteria. Other people suggested Caryll had perpetrated a wicked hoax in order to attract the attention of the small world that surrounded her. From that time on, she was regarded with open suspicion as a neurotic—someone whose illness was psychosomatic. Whatever the cause of her illness, this event had a tremendous impact on the rest of her life. Never again did she experience such intense suffering, and the memory of it led her to be acutely sensitive to people who experience anxiety neurosis. She was convinced that the cure is allowing oneself to be "touched by God" through another human being. In her case, this was accomplished through the priest who brought her holy communion. This surrender to God was more than the abandonment of oneself to God's will or the acceptance of suffering. It was giving oneself up to God in order to be transformed, as the bread and wine on the altar are changed into Christ. She wrote toward the end of her life:

> In this surrender is, I believe, the cure for the torment of self, which is precisely what most psychological suffering is. It is the cure for the weakness that cannot carry the common burden of the world's sin, the cure for the fear that causes the will to wither before the challenge of life, the cure for the feebleness that makes the impact of natural beauty painful, the cure for the cowardice that causes the heart to contract and shrink before the challenge of love.[4]

We understand today that an experience such as Caryll's, especially early in life, carries within it the seeds of healing and transformation and an invitation to greatness of soul and a larger sense of life. Many who have suffered such wounding at about the same age that

28

Caryll did become healers of body, mind and spirit. In Caryll's case, she became able to see the Christ-self lying dormant in others, and, in calling that part of them to life, she enabled them to become both whole and holy.

> The beginning of human happiness, and even of human sanity, is to begin to know God....Goodness draws the human soul as a tide is drawn by light.[5]

Exercise 2.1 Images

Materials needed: *journals, paper and pens.*
Approximate time: *25 minutes.*
Script for Guide: Before we learned a language, we thought in images. When we assign a name to something, we no longer experience it directly. We see a chair, and instead of noticing its actual shape, form, color and texture, we jump to the generic word for it. Because many of the images that have impacted our lives become unconscious, we think that we live out of beliefs and concepts. In the story of Caryll and the sermon on mortal sin, the preacher used language to paint a powerful word picture, one that filled the tiny, lonely, and oversensitive child with terror. No amount of reasoning, not even the sacrament of confession, was able to free her from a state of anxiety. Her cure came from replacing a dark image with the healing image of light and union with Christ in holy communion. Caryll had an uncanny ability to create just the right image in her writings later in life. Among them were the green sap rising in the branches, the coat worn to the shape of its owner, the poor little bird in its cage, dark crimson scars blazing like dancing stars.

Take some time now to reconnect with the images that have shaped and are shaping your life, whether for good or for ill. If you are working alone, you may want to read the following script into a cassette player and then listen to it, allowing it to evoke awareness of the images present in the depths of your being.

Find a place to sit—either in a straight chair or on the floor. Make sure that your spine is erect. One way to do this is to imagine your head suspended from the ceiling by a rope or thread. Keeping your spine erect helps to prevent you from falling asleep. Then, turn your attention toward your breath. Focusing on the breath is an ancient method for entering into a meditative state. Continuing to breathe, allow your breath to find its own pace. Allow your thoughts to come to rest. Without trying to think in any particular way, just allow your thoughts to enter consciousness and float away. As you continue to breathe in and out, allow your tongue to rest quietly, pressed gently against your top front teeth. As you inhale and exhale, allow any tension in your body to relax.

In this quiet place, all the chaotic thoughts and emotions that dance wildly within us most of the time come to rest. Relax and enjoy the experience of an empty, clear, uncluttered mind and a heart whose emotions are at rest. Remaining in the stillness, become aware of the fact that emptiness refills itself. Images, memories, feelings, intuitive hunches and bodily sensations begin to bubble up from your depths. Like the images of a dream, they carry messages in symbolic form about your life, images from your childhood and patterns that have shaped your behavior and your beliefs about life and about God. Observe and record with pen or pencil, without judging, without censoring, whatever surfaces. Pay attention to the inner events bubbling up from your depths and record them in the peaceful atmosphere of silence.

Exercise 2.2 Sacred Wounds[6]

Materials: *A bell or chime to mark times of transition.*
Approximate time: *One hour and forty-five minutes.*
Script for Guide: This is an exercise in the healing of emotional, psychological and spiritual wounding. Its purpose is to come to a new way of seeing a past event, to discover the blessing in the wounding, and to be transformed by a new understanding of its meaning in our life. We honor the sacredness of this experience by committing ourselves to confidentiality. Nothing we hear is to be shared with others, either here or beyond the confines of the sacred space we have created. Although this exercise may be therapeutic, we need to remind ourselves that we are not acting as therapists. The process is designed to go beyond analysis, interpretation or comforting each other. We sit in high witness, posing questions to our partner and listening intently. We keep what we are tempted to reply to ourselves. Begin by finding a partner, preferably someone not well known to you. Then decide who will be the first to pose the questions and who will respond. Sit facing each other and allow several minutes of silence to reflect upon the times of wounding in your life.

I am going to dictate a series of questions to you. The person sitting in high witness, in the place of Christ, will repeat each question after I present it. The person answering the questions will have five minutes to reply to each one. If you are finished before the five minutes are up, repeat the question and go more deeply into the story the questions evoke.

1. How were you wounded?
2. How did you respond to this experience of wounding?
3. What were the consequences of this wounding in your life, both for good and for ill?
4. In the light of telling your story, what have you come to realize? What patterns or larger story do you see playing themselves out in your life?
5. How has or how might your wounding enable you to serve others?

When both partners have had a turn, move on to the next step.
You have been telling your stories on a personal and an historical level. Now tell them again from the point of view of the Larger Story—as a myth, or a fairy tale. Begin by telling your story in the third person, speaking of yourself as "she," "he" or "it." You may personify yourself as an animal or a fictional character. Allow your story to rise up from your depths without trying consciously to create it. It helps to begin with "Once upon a time there was...." Try not to judge, censor or edit what comes to you. If you are the listener, try to be fully present without commenting upon or discussing what you hear. Begin by saying to your partner, "Tell me your story, beginning with 'Once upon a time.'"

Allow fifteen minutes for each partner to tell his or her story. Ring a bell or sound a chime to mark when it is time to switch roles. Invite each pair to close this exercise with a blessing.

Now, to bring this exercise to a close, let us bless each other, using a simple gesture or a short prayer. This is your opportunity to respond to what you have heard, to affirm one another, and to encourage each other. You may want to speak while placing your hands on each other's shoulders and looking kindly into each other's eyes. Do whatever is most comfortable for you.

Group process: *Some time needs to be allowed to process this experience either in the group, or by allowing time for the participants to write in their journals. You can ask simple questions such as "How are you?" or "How was this experience for you?"*

For those working alone: *Answer the questions in writing and then create a story or fairy tale that takes your experience to a level beyond the individual and personal.*

Prayer

> Lord Jesus, nailed to the Cross,
> help us to see the flames of new life
> shining forth from our very wounds
> to give us strength in weakness
> and light in the dark shadows of our lives.

Chapter 3:
The Betrayal of Trust

Come, let us walk for a time among ghosts and memories.
Let us forget that not only home was lost,
not only Father and Mother
(Home,
and Father
and Mother
were God).[1]

One day, shortly after Caryll had celebrated her ninth birthday, the family's housemaid Beatrice announced to her amid loud and strangled sobs that Caryll's parents were getting a divorce. Although her parents had been estranged for a long time, they never quarreled in her presence, so the shock must have been enormous. Beatrice added that from then on, Caryll would be no better off than an orphan in a foundling home, indeed worse off, since no one in this world wanted her at all. Imagine being told that no one wants you. Even to a child who felt unloved, this would be a terrible realization. As most children do, Caryll had identified her parents with God. They stood for security, home, refuge, food, warmth and light. Now her trust in them suddenly seemed to have been misplaced. How could she trust God?

Caryll went to the box room at the top of the house where she had built an altar out of empty, twisted toothpaste tubes. She had placed a crude holy card of the crucifixion on this altar, and it was to this secret place that she brought her disillusionment. Kneeling before the altar, she vowed to the crucified Christ that she would harden her heart and from this time on would belong only to herself. Looking at this event in retrospect, Caryll realized as an adult that this armor was as brittle as the shell of a bird's egg, but it served her for the moment.

Caryll's parents placed their girls in a French convent boarding school called Snow Hill in a suburb of Birmingham. Caryll expected the town to be covered with snowflakes, white and glittering like a fairy story. Her disillusionment in the gray and dreary town only added to her state. She described herself as "hard and sour as a green apple, eaten up with self-pity and in revolt against the whole world."[2]

The convent re-enchanted her, however, with its austere beauty, shining cleanliness and the simplicity of having only what is essential. She found God in the white linen sheet on her bed, the touch of cold water, the morning light on the white dormitory curtains and in the very air she breathed. The sisters seemed to radiate the love of God; some even burned with it.

This convent school was a refuge for the children of divorce or from unhappy homes. The maternal care and love the sisters gave to Caryll healed her of the terrible wound of becoming an orphan while her parents were still alive. Holidays came and went, but her parents did not bring her home. She lived in the convent like a little postulant, joining the sisters for recreation and helping them pit plums for jam. The cloister became her home. She walked in the garden with the superior of the community and collected eggs with a lay sister responsible for much of the manual labor. There were times for fasting and times for feasting. She especially recalled eating bananas for breakfast on holy days, special sweets at recreation and Sister Martha of the Holy Shroud telling the children lurid stories of the suffering souls in purgatory while she did her darning in the evening.

If she were alive today, Caryll would probably describe her experience of placement in the French convent as abandonment. Her disillusionment was greater than that of a child who discovers that there is no Santa Claus and wonders if everyone has lied about Jesus too. Our primary reaction to betrayal or abandonment may be a determination never to trust anyone again. Another reaction is self-isolation. Trust and betrayal are contained in each other. In our closest relationships we experience the greatest agony of betrayal: the child who is ridiculed in front of strangers, the friend who discloses a confidence, the husband who leaves his wife for a younger woman, the associate who drops out of a project. How do we keep from becoming hard, cynical, vengeful or paranoid in the face of such circumstances? How do we keep from saying, "It doesn't matter anyhow?" One way is to realize, usually after the distance that the passage of time affords, how a tragic event has in fact been a happy fault. Through suffering we are opened to a larger life and greatness of soul. The heart of Christ's message is that we must die to self in order to be born to eternal life. When Jesus' primal trust in his

Father was broken and he cried, "My God, my God, why have you forsaken me?" he entered fully into the human condition. In doing so, he made a fuller life in the Spirit possible for all of us. It is only in the cracking of the seed that the little plant can grow and blossom.

> Remember that it is at the sore place, and only there, that our healing begins; and that whenever healing does begin at a sore which you have had the courage and love to expose, there, in that sore spot, the healing of the whole world begins.[3]

Exercise 3.1 The Healing of Betrayal and Loss of Trust[4]

Materials needed: *A box of tissues and a CD or cassette player. CD or cassette album:* Bones *by Gabrielle Roth and the Mirrors (Red Bank, NJ: The Moving Center, 1989).* Bones *is a musical lament for the past and a prayer for the future.*

Sacred space: *adequate to move around in easily with a dusk-like atmosphere.*

Approximate time: *Two hours, including a fifteen-minute break.*

Script for Guide: We are going to explore the role of abandonment and betrayal in our own lives. In this partner exercise, confidentiality is essential. We are to respect what we hear and to refrain from repeating it to anyone. In an exercise on betrayal, the last thing we want is to be betrayed by our partner. We also need to commit ourselves to staying with this exercise until the very end, so that another experience of abandonment is not added to anyone's life. Choose a partner, preferably someone you do not know very well, and then find a place where you will stand together.

Make sure the room is cleared of unnecessary furniture and other obstacles.

You are going to take turns remembering times in your lives when you experienced betrayal or abandonment. Each person will go through the entire process, so decide who will begin, who will be the questioner and compassionate listener and who will be the one who answers. As you begin, stand and face each other. Put your hands on each other's shoulders. Close your eyes and for a few minutes enter into great moaning and groaning about the great betrayals and times of abandonment in your lives. Don't be shy. Let your anguish out. Howl like wolves if you like.

Allow at least two or three minutes.

Now, you who are to ask the questions, open your eyes and stand as guide and high witness to your partner. You, who are about to remember, keep your eyes closed. Your partner is going to guide you around the room in a manner that will enable you to walk backward from the present into the past.

Make sure there is enough room so that each pair can move about the room without constant concern about bumping into others.

As you move backward, feel time entering you through your back and recall the occasions in your life when someone betrayed your trust or abandoned you: the times you discovered that someone had lied to you, the times someone broke a promise, the times someone accused you falsely, the times you felt left behind, the times you felt rejected, the times you felt unseen and unheard. Each time a memory comes to you, stop and relate the story to your guide.

You who are the guide, walk in a loving and supportive manner. Avoid bumping into others or into objects in the room. Try to make your partner feel that you can be trusted to do no harm. When your partner speaks, listen compassionately and attentively. Avoid making comments or entering into a discussion. Honor your partner's right to be heard without being questioned or comforted. You stand in the place of the crucified Christ on the altar to whom Caryll Houselander poured out the pain in her nine-year-old heart.

Start the music as soon as the pairs begin to move. Keep the volume low for this part of the process so that those who are speaking can be heard easily.

You who are moving backward through your life, be aware of the moment when you have come to a key event. Your bodily reactions and your emotions will be so strong that you will realize this is a major occasion of betrayal or abandonment. At this point, you and your guide may sit down and wait in silence for the next step.

Continue this process until you notice that everyone is seated.

I am going to pose a series of questions now. I will allow adequate time after each question for the guide to repeat it and then listen to the answer. So let us begin.

Allow about five minutes for each answer. Stop when most pairs are ready to move ahead.

1. Tell me how you were betrayed.

When you notice that partners have begun to chat rather than speak and listen, you may want to say, "Stay focused on your partner as a compassionate listener. Be careful not to shift the focus to yourself and your experiences. Avoid giving advice or comfort."

2. How did you feel at the time?

3. What has happened in your life as a result, both for good and for ill? (For *example,* "How are you different from the way you might have been if this had never happened? Often we only look at the scars, the bad things. Try to be aware of something good, too.")

4. In the light of what you have just shared, what have you come to realize? What patterns are playing themselves out in your life? What do you see now that you haven't realized earlier?

5. In the light of sharing, what meaning can you give to the experience? What is the larger story?

6. Now I want you to tell me the whole story in mythic or fairy-tale form. Tell the story in the third person. Allow the story to go beyond the wounding to some kind of healing or happy ending.

You may want to explain this further by giving an example:

If Caryll Houselander were retelling her story, she might say, "Once upon a time there was a little girl with red hair and a very strong will who was born into a family that was rather well off but somewhat eccentric. Her parents did not pay much attention to her and often left her home alone with the servants. Shortly after her ninth birthday, one of the housemaids, who had a tendency to wail, announced between great sobs that her parents had decided to get a divorce. Furthermore, neither one of them wanted to be bothered with her at all, so they were placing her in a boarding school run by nuns from a foreign country. She was so upset (mostly because she hadn't suspected that her parents didn't get along) that she ran upstairs to the attic, where she had built a secret little altar. She poured out her heart to a picture of Jesus on the Cross. She told him that she would never love or trust anyone again and that she would harden her heart so that no one would ever hurt her like this. Once she arrived at the school, however, the warm, motherly love of one of the sisters broke right through the fragile shell she had built to protect herself. Before long she felt at home in the boarding school and did not mind at all that she could not go home for the holidays as the other children did. At least, that's what she told herself. Later in life, she was able to help many children who felt unwanted and unloved to find happiness.

Whatever story you tell, allow it to well up from your depths rather than trying to create it consciously or deliberately. This will allow your connection to a larger story to emerge. Allow yourself to be surprised by what comes out of your mouth. Listeners, remember to stay present without engaging in any discussion or response!

After ten or fifteen minutes take a fifteen-minute break. It helps to warn participants that you are approaching closure. For example, "You have two minutes to allow your story to come to completion." *When participants return, invite them to trade places and repeat the same process.*

Group process: *Afterward, process the experience either with a general discussion of what has happened or in small groups. Then allow time for individual journal entries.*

41

For those working alone: *Write a dialogue with a person you trust. Hear that person asking the questions in the exercise above and record your answers. Then write your story in fairy-tale form.*

Reflect upon the emotions and memories that are evoked as you do this and record what you have learned from this exercise.

Prayer

> In the dark
> and the cold,
> I believe
> in the green leaf.
> In the frost
> and the hard crust,
> I hope
> in the flower.
> In the cold winter,
> unloving,
> I love.[5]

Chapter 4:
Smoky

Mr. Bower was seated down
In the court in wig and gown.
His face was hot and fiery red,
With perspiration on his head.
He was the finest in the Court,
So our noble Judge Bray thought.
Occasionally he had a joke,
But wisely and bravely Bower spoke.
The words he spoke went straight to the heart,
And he won his case with skillful art.[1]

With the near-extinction of the extended family, greater mobility and the frequent occurrence of divorce in today's society, many more children suffer as Caryll did. We are prone to blame the circumstances of our childhood for our unskilled behavior as adults. How was Caryll able to give love to others so freely as an adult when she had been starved for affection as a child herself? Possibly the answer lies in the person of George Spencer Bower, a close family friend who had no children of his own. Caryll described him as the most lovable person in her life. From the time she was a little child, he played with her and, informally, he taught her practically everything she knew. It appears that her formal schooling was both brief and ineffective. She could neither spell nor compose a decent sentence. By the time she was fifteen, she knew no more, except about religion and painting, than Smoky had taught her. She continued to look to him as a mentor and friend until his death on January 20, 1929. On that occasion she recorded in her journal, "Smoky has died. I am happy for him and long to die and be with him again."[2]

Not everyone loved Smoky as Caryll did. Evidently he was irritable, disconcertingly outspoken and honest, and did not suffer fools gladly. Although he did not tolerate children who were spoiled or pampered, he seems to have excepted his relationship with Caryll from this rule. He was a fine lawyer and an author of legal textbooks. On special occasions, he took Caryll to court to hear him plead a case. Married to a daughter of an actor, he loved the theater and took Caryll to every kind of play. They sat in the royal box to watch Shakespeare and other plays for grownups, not children. Sometimes he took her backstage, adding to the excitement. Annually, they went to see *Peter Pan*. As they drove home through Hyde Park, Smoky would tell her that they were passing through Never-Never Land.

Caryll lay awake at night, trembling and sweating as she recalled scenes from *Macbeth*—the groans of old King Duncan, the fearful chattering of the daggers in Macbeth's hands and the ghastly little ghosts who rose from a kind of giant cauldron in the green limelight during the banquet scene. In spite of this, when Smoky came home in the evening, she would act scenes from *Macbeth* for him. She described herself in these acting roles as a hideous child with a squint, but with rather remarkable long, thick carroty hair, which I suppose fitted me for the part of Lady Macbeth. I was particularly fond of playing the sleepwalking scene, but hindered from giving it the full dramatic force that I should have liked to do by Smoky's little dog, Spot, who, used to nothing but gentleness and welcome from Smoky and me, would look bewildered and startled at the words, "Out, damned Spot!"[3]

Smoky taught her not only love for the theater, but also love for poetry: in English for the sense and sound, and in Greek simply for the music of the words. He instructed her in English law, insisting it had been based upon the Ten Commandments. He believed that justice was a basic and essential virtue for everyone. He taught her philosophy, reading Socrates and practically all of Plato to her. He taught her to believe in God, but also in the existence of angels and fairies. In her book, *Guilt,* Caryll chastised parents for not allowing their children to read myths and fairy tales. She believed that children need to fantasize and to read stories that contain within them both the darkness and danger of the forest where the wicked witch lives and the light breaking through as Prince Charming rescues Sleeping Beauty. She saw Christ in disguise in the hero of every fairy story. Whether the son of a king or a beggar, he goes out to face evil, strikes off the seven heads of the dragon, returns with wounds that shine like jewels and claims the bride his bravery has won. He is both savior and lover.

Caryll bemoaned the fact that we live in a world of disenchantment, a world that blinds us to the sheer loveliness of our surroundings. Today the re-enchantment of the world is a popular topic, but in the materialism of her times, only the proven facts of science and technology were considered real. She wrote that we go through life with dark forces within us and around us, haunted by the ghosts of repudiated terrors and embarrassments, assailed by devils. She added that we do not realize invisible hands guide us and many flames pierce the darkness, from night-lights to the stars. Those who fear looking into their own hearts know nothing of the light that shines in the darkness.[4]

When it was in its infancy, Caryll foresaw the potential television might have to alienate us from ourselves and from each other as we sit staring stupidly at the screen. Her childhood was filled with games that required playfulness and the art of storytelling. Smoky played cricket with Ruth and Caryll when he visited them at home during the holidays. He read enchanting stories to them and taught them fascinating things about history. But perhaps the most exciting game he played with them was called, "What was this in the olden times?" They would go on walks or to the beach and bring something they found to him with that question. Then he would respond. Just imagine Caryll bringing a little pebble of glass frosted by the ocean, a "sea jewel," to him. Hear her say, "Smoky, what was this in the olden times?" and listen to what he might have said:

> *This sea jewel began as grains of sand on a beach in Spain. It was taken to a factory, where it was melted in a fire and blown into a glass bottle. For a long time it was used at the sumptuous banquets of a wealthy man. Full, rich wines were poured into the cups of his guests from it. The wine had*

come from distant vineyards near Rome where the sun ripened the grapes to just the right flavor. In the olden days, glass was not as clear as it is today. It was like my name, Smoky. There was a man named Paul, an apostle of Jesus, who spoke of "seeing through a glass darkly." People couldn't see their images in mirrors as we do now, either. Their faces were dim and distorted.

The wine had been brought to the wealthy man on old wooden boats rowed by galley slaves. One day, a magnificent Spanish galleon with its white, red, and purple sails like the wings of great birds moored in a harbor nearby. The wealthy man sold the captain some wine in this bottle, and from there it traveled to the shores of England with the Spanish Armada. You may remember what year that was. Yes, 1588! One of the ships, hit by a huge cannonball, tossed and turned as it burned. Then an incredible storm came up and the ship washed upon some cragged rocks along the English shore. The bottle was broken in the raging seas and the continual action of the waves, the salt water and sand on the chips of glass made them smooth and round as you see this one today.

For hundreds of years, mermaids played with the "sea jewels" and made bracelets and necklaces from them. They spent most of the day combing their long golden hair, and the sound of their songs lured sailors to jump overboard and swim to the bottom of the ocean looking for them. You can still hear their voices if you put your ear to a large seashell. Perhaps tomorrow we can look for one and listen to their songs. But now, let me return to my story. The moon, a bright spirit, scattered her silver radiance over the waves and drew the dark waters of the sea toward the shore and back again, creating what we know as tides. These tides eventually carried your "sea jewel" to the shore where you found it today!

This story illustrates how Smoky might have improvised as he went along, embellishing his stories with both fact and fiction. He moved from the description of a particular object to how it was made and how it was used. Then he went back further and further into the history of all objects that were like it to the universal, mythic level.

Improvisation, whether it be in music, the theater, dance, or any other activity, connects us to that which goes beyond the self and our individual life. It takes us beyond time into the eternal stream of ongoing creativity. Pure free play allows us to explore and to do something for its own sake, for the sheer pleasure and joy of it. A kind of spiritual connection happens in this kind of play. Playing together in this fashion, we enter into the possibility of listening, watching and sensing in common, in community. We let go of being in control and allow ourselves to "go with the flow." We develop a mutual awareness, a consideration and a trust that bring us to a subtle attunement with each other. We move in harmony, as jazz musicians do. Although each plays his or her instrument, they all find a common rhythm and harmony. Take some time now to let the child in you come to life and play once again.

Exercise 4.1. "What Was This in the Olden Times?"

Materials needed: *Either have participants go on a scavenger hunt, or have available a collection of diverse small objects from which they can choose (for example, hairpins, pieces of wood and glass, used toys, nails, screws). You may want to play children's music in the background, songs such as "Pop Goes the Weasel" and "London Bridge Is Falling Down."*

Approximate time: *Forty-five minutes.*

Script for Guide: Take your object and find a partner. Sit down facing each other. You are going to take turns asking each other the same question Caryll and her sister Ruth asked Smoky. Hold the object up so that your partner can see it, and then ask, "What was this in the olden times?" Your partner has fifteen minutes to tell you the story of your object, using as much history and fantasy as possible in relation to it.

Announce when the fifteen minutes are over. Ringing a bell or a chime helps.

Now trade places, and the one who asked the question first becomes the storyteller.

Group process: *When both partners have had enough time to tell their story, process this experience either in pairs or in the group. Do not be rigid about periods. Children absorbed in play are not bound by the clock. Any parent who has tried to call a child from play to eat supper knows this. Even though children might "just" be playing, they do not want to come to the table until they have finished what they are doing. Ask what this* *experience was like for each person. What happened when they told their stories?*

For those working alone: *Find a stone, an old bead, a piece of clothing or some other object and write a story about it. Go back into its history. Where did it come from? How was it made? As you move back through history, create tales about the people and things that were part of its creation. Afterward, journal about your inner experiences as you wrote this story.*

Exercise 4.2. Free Play 1

Materials needed: *Paper and pencil for journal work. A large space free of obstacles.*

Approximate time: *Thirty minutes.*

Script for Guide: Play is at the heart of all creative and spiritual activity. A prerequisite for play is the freedom to enter into it spontaneously. A simple way to learn just how free you are is to enter into play with two other people. Stand facing each other in what would be the corners of a triangle. Spend a minute breathing together and looking at each other to establish contact. Then any one of the three may initiate playing. The other two "Follow the Leader" until one of them decides to initiate something else. That person then becomes the leader. Any one of the three can change the direction of play at any time. You may do anything you want (within reason). Jump. Run in place. Gesture. Make faces. Hold hands and spin around. Act like monkeys. Bark like dogs. Allow your imagination to run wild.

Five minutes ought to be sufficient for this exercise. If you notice one person in a triad leading for too long, encourage the others in the threesome to lead.

Group process: *Allow five or ten minutes after this exercise for reflection upon this experience and journal writing. Invite those who wish to share what happened to them. It may have become apparent that one person in the triad needed to be in control at all times and found it difficult to follow others. On the other hand, some may have hesitated to become the leader. This is a good piece of self-knowledge that can be transferred to many aspects of life. Often if this exercise is done for a sufficient length of time, all three begin to do the same thing almost simultaneously. We refer to this as becoming entrained. The same phenomenon can be observed in a group beating drums or rhythm sticks. In the beginning, there is a cacophony of sound. Unless the group is composed entirely of people who are accustomed to marching to their own drums, they find themselves beating in unison after a few minutes.*[5]

Exercise 4.3 Free Play II

Materials needed: *Peppy marching music. A large space free of obstacles.*

Approximate time: *Thirty minutes.*

Script for Guide: *Begin with the entire group marching around the room.*

Listen to the music. What images or actions does it evoke? Become whatever comes to you: an airplane flying through the sky, a washing machine churning, a mother rocking her baby in a crib or pushing a swing.

Now become a fish swimming through the water. Notice how it feels to be able to breathe under water and to move effortlessly as you move your tail and fins and move with the current. Slowly feel that you are turning into a frog. Notice how this differs from being a fish. You can swim under water and you can hop on land. What do you eat? What do you have to watch out for in order to stay alive? What kind of sounds can you make? Slowly you turn into a reptile. Where do you find yourself? What are you? How do you move? Show us. Suddenly you become a little mammal, a furry thing that crawls on all fours. Show us how you move. Let us hear what sounds you make. How do you feel? Now find yourself becoming a monkey. You can leap from branch to branch in the trees and hang by one leg or your tail. You can romp around and stand up on your hind legs. Notice the change in your emotional state and your field of vision. What can you see? What do you hear? What do you enjoy doing? Show us. And now you are a great ape. How does it feel to be in an ape's body? How does the world around you look? What do you like to eat? Show us. Now, gradually, you are becoming a Neanderthal. How are you different from the apes? Show us how you walk and what you are doing. And now you find yourself becoming a human being at the beginning of the twenty-first century. You are part of a three-ring circus. What part are you playing? The ringmaster? A clown? A tightrope walker? An acrobat? Many acts are going on at once. Be aware of what others are doing. You are becoming one great cast in the theater of life. Begin to interact with each other until you form one body performing in unison. When the music stops, you may take a bow and find a seat.

Allow several minutes for each stage of this exercise and at least five minutes for the final act. Watch to see if everyone is participating and moving toward a single act. Are some going off alone? Are some doing their own thing? Do not stop them. Just be aware of what is happening.

Group process: *When everyone is seated, feed back what you have noticed. Ask them what the experience was like for them and how they feel right now.*

For those working alone: *Record the Script for Guide on a tape cassette. Since you are alone, you will not be able to interact with others, but you can use your imagination. When you have finished the exercise, take a few minutes to reflect upon your experience and write about it in your journal. Note what stages were the most memorable for you.*

Exercise 4.4 Mentors and Mentoring

Materials needed: *Question sheets and pens.*
Approximate time: *Thirty minutes.*
Script for Guide: Caryll was blessed with a loving and wise mentor in her life from early childhood until the age of twenty-eight. As an adult, she cared for and mentored several children, especially Joan, the daughter of her friend Iris Wyndham. Caryll and Iris, a divorcee, lived together from about 1923 until Caryll's death. Caryll saw that motherhood was a vocation even for women who had no children of their own. What is essential is the capacity for love, to be awake and alive. She wrote that in

many people the Christ child is ignored and lacks proper nurturing. The Christ in us needs a mother so that we are not suffocated by worldliness and the temptation to compromise with faith and holiness. Without this inner mother to counsel and make strong the Christ-life in us, we may never become more than a sickly colorless flower growing in a dark cellar.[6]

Form small groups and share with each other who, other than your parents, were the significant people in your lives. Spend some time reflecting on the questions before you begin to share. Questions may be duplicated.

1. Who played with you, listened to you and answered your questions? An aunt or an uncle, a grandparent, a friend of the family, a teacher, a pastor?

2. How did they influence you and help you to become who you are today?

3. How are you being or could you be this kind of mentor for a young child now?

For those working alone: *Write in your journal about a person or several persons who had a significant impact upon you as a child. Then reflect upon and write about the ways in which you are or could be that wise person, that person who fosters the Christ-life in some child now.*

Prayer

> Come, let us pray
> that we gently nurture the seed of life
> in every man, woman, and child we meet,
> especially those who hold what they could become
> in their hands like a fragile flower.

Chapter 5:
The Seeking

If, instead of using the expression "spiritual life," we used "the seeking," we should set out from the beginning and go on to the end with a clearer idea of what our life with God will be on this earth; and we should be less vulnerable, that is to say, less easily shattered by disillusionment and discouragement.[1]

Smoky's strong belief that the Roman Catholic Church was the one founded by Jesus Christ stayed with Caryll during her long search for a spiritual home as a young adult. He had based his proofs upon the evidence of the gospels, applying the searching methods of a lawyer to support his arguments. The fact that the church had survived all the corruption assailing it in the course of history was enough to convince him that it was sustained by God, not by the hierarchy or membership. His favorite point was that Catholicism was all-inclusive, including all that is beautiful and good in any other religion. In spite of his influence in regard to its authenticity, Caryll knew little about the teachings of the Catholic Church. She had attended Catholic schools, but she had learned little about Christian doctrine and practice. Her analytical, hypercritical and inquisitive mind led her to be perplexed by the inconsistencies between her experience of life and the teachings of the church. Her religion teacher accused her of insolence because of her constant questions.

Throughout her life, Caryll was deeply sensitive and suffered from a panoply of maladies: headaches, toothaches and often sheer exhaustion. She was a picky eater. Not all of her complaints were unjustified, however. When her uncle examined her because she had difficulty eating, he discovered that she had been living with a diseased appendix.

After her recovery from an appendix operation, Caryll was sent to a boarding school run by an order of English sisters. The girls there were very active in sports. Feelings of inadequacy and loneliness led her to act superior to her classmates and to refuse to play in or to pray for their competitions. She also criticized the sisters. Sometimes she would ventilate by writing verses to her teddy bear, Roosey, a lifelong companion. She also poured out her contempt for her classmates and teachers in letters to Smoky. On one occasion, the sister who was prefect returned a letter Caryll had written to him. She spoke to Caryll gently and without anger. "I won't let this go because I cannot allow you to say such unkind things about the children that I love. I love them and Our Lord loves them." Then in reference to what Caryll had said about "Mother So-and-So," the Prefect said, "About myself, you are right. I *am* the cock of the walk here, so there is nothing to be done about that but to make the best of it." Shamed, Caryll rewrote the letter. The sister took this letter and sealed it without reading it. She told Caryll that from then on she would be allowed the needed outlet of uncensored correspondence with Smoky. She could hand in letters to him sealed and receive his unopened.

Evidently Smoky could be as outspoken and forthright with Caryll as he was with everyone. He answered her, writing that it was she who wanted the jam without the bread, the poetry and peace of religion but not its discipline. Because of the honesty in his letters, Caryll began to see the truth. The girls who were her classmates had been unusually kind to her in spite of her uncharitable attitude toward them. With the help of the sister and Smoky, Caryll was prevented from becoming hateful and hardhearted. This was Caryll's last chance to choose a healthy attitude toward others and toward life itself. Dr. Paley, a friend of the family, had recommended the school as preventive medicine. "If you don't adjust to life now, you will become a chronic invalid," he said to Caryll.

Just when she had finally settled down and had begun to feel at home there, Caryll received a letter from her mother telling her that at the end of the term, about a week's time, she was to come home. Caryll's education ended abruptly, barely after it had begun in earnest. She discovered the reason when she arrived in London. The priest who had given her *viaticum* as a child had left his religious order to become a secular priest, and now he was quite ill. He had moved into her mother's boarding house, causing quite a scandal. Caryll's job was to take care of him and to help with the housework. Almost all of Caryll's Catholic friends refused to associate with her because of the priest. She continued to visit Dr. Paley's family at the admonition of Smoky, who told her it would hurt them deeply if she refused their invitations. Caryll was shocked that good Catholics who were active in the church could be so cruel and vindictive toward someone they regarded as a sinner. She became aware of the fact that those who profess no faith can be more Christian than those who are Catholic.

During the years she worked for her mother, Caryll often thought about skipping Mass on Sunday. The break came one Sunday when she had made a heroic effort to attend Mass. She had had to work that morning. Since Mass schedules were not as convenient then as they are now, she walked across London to the only church that had a service at noon. This church still maintained the practice of pew rent. She didn't have a penny to her name. By the time she arrived, all the free seats were taken, so she slipped into an empty place among the "sixpennys." She had scarcely knelt down when the usher prodded her in the ribs with the collection basket. "Sixpence," he said, poking her again. She looked up and shook her head.

"Sixpence," he repeated, continuing to prod her.

"I haven't got a sixpence," she whispered.

"All right then, you must go into the free seats," he said.

"There isn't one," she replied.

"Well, then, sixpence."

As a priest standing in the aisle watched, Caryll sprang up and pushed her way out of the seat. "You are not going, child?" he said. She shook him off and replied, "Yes, I am, and I will never come to Mass again!" She began her long walk home hardly able to stop tears of rage. She kept her promise for years.

Many people would have just stopped going to church, but something drove Caryll to look for a new spiritual home. She questioned many Anglican priests, high, evangelical and low church. She went to their services, drawn to the hymn singing of those marked by the more emotional expressions of Christianity. She found that they provided a certain relief from nervous tension. It did not seem that it mattered to them what you *believed* as long as you *felt* good. She experienced emotional delight in the Wesleyan chapels, and she had to hold on to the bench at the Salvation Army meetings to keep herself from being swept forth in a wave of hysteria to "testify." No two clergymen answered her many questions the same way. So she turned from Christianity to explore Buddhism and Judaism. She was particularly impressed by the story a Buddhist friend told her. He and his brothers bought fourteen golden bells, each named after one of them, and hung them in the Burmese jungle. When the wind stirred, the bells rang out prayers for their deceased mother. Caryll found the symbolism of golden bells ringing out prayers that only God and the wild beasts could hear more beautiful than the traditional Buddhist prayer wheels. She described this friend, however, as the laziest man in the world. His prayer was like that of Catholics who light candles in church, she thought.

Caryll escaped from working in her mother's boarding house by applying for a scholarship to an art school. Eventually she moved into her own apartment. One of the cleverest students in her art class, aware of her spiritual homelessness, put her in touch with a rabbi. Although he showed little use for her, he agreed to give her several instructions in the Jewish faith. Caryll went to the synagogue several times with his niece. There was something fierce and terrible about the Jewish liturgy, Caryll found, but something familiar too. It was through her exploration of Judaism that Caryll become increasingly convinced that Christ was a seed sown in Israel that had flowered in the Catholic Church. It seemed that each religion she studied had something of truth and beauty. "Did the Catholic Church include everything?" she asked. Her own testimony reveals a struggle between *wanting and not wanting* to be Catholic.

One last foray led her to the Russian Orthodox Church. She had many Russian friends, refugees from the revolution. Both those who practiced their faith and those who didn't seemed to her to be more sincerely Christian than any other people she had met. She was drawn to their emphasis on what she called "the humiliated Christ." He was not perfect. According to legend, he was lame and had limped across Russia from time to time throughout history. She also loved the beauty of their liturgy. However, Smoky explained the rift that had occurred between the Eastern and Western churches in the eleventh century and convinced her that the Orthodox Christians were just as schismatic as the Anglo-Catholics. Thus she remained a spiritual orphan, refusing to return to the Catholic Church but finding no other religion to take its place.

This period of Caryll's life marks the transition from a life of faith largely imposed by the adults in her life to one based upon her own inner experiences. During such in-between times, when the old is no more and what is to come is not yet, we have the opportunity to relate simply as human beings apart from beliefs, roles or status.

Caryll found greater freedom among her bohemian friends of the world of art. They seemed to practice more charity and humanity than her former Roman Catholic companions. However, Caryll missed the church's rituals, especially those that were communal in nature. Rituals keep us connected to our own depths, to each other, to the earth and to the larger patterns in the universe. They help bring our inner and outer lives into harmony. It was only by attending Mass regularly that Caryll had been able to sustain her longing for God and her awareness of the divine presence. Those who knew her noted that two Carylls seemed to coexist. One seemed to be continually aware of the divine. The other was hysterically funny, used strong language, told off-color jokes and smoked heavily.

When Caryll finished studying art, she earned her living decorating churches and children's nurseries. She worked occasionally as a commercial artist. When she did not make enough money through her art, she resorted to writing love letters for people, working as a scrubwoman, taking care of children and traveling with a troupe of actors. Her acting career consisted of making sounds offstage such as those of a rooster crowing and a husband and wife quarreling. She also wrote plays from time to time and invited her mother and friends to join her in putting on performances. Deep down, Caryll longed to be a poet. By the time Caryll arrived at her room at night, however, she was too cold, hungry and tired to write. So she sat in the dark and listened.

> I heard the tap, tap, tap of a blind man's stick passing below in the street. It had an extraordinary effect on me. Somehow, between me and this

unknown blind man there was an affinity. Was I not spiritually blind? Was I not, too, tapping here, there, and everywhere, longing for the light, but feeling my way in darkness, because the darkness was not in the night that was lit by the splendor of stars, but in my own soul?[2]

Caryll began to pray for this blind man, a habit she had almost lost by this time. She also felt the urge to go out and walk among the crowds in the evening. She wanted to rub shoulders with the people in the London streets and, in a way she could not define, take part in their lives. Her favorite route was a sordid road, not only because everyone there seemed to be intensely alive, but also because the smells from the fish and chips bars took away her smallest desire for food. From there she walked to Hyde Park where she discovered the Catholic Evidence Guild. She thought it was another kind of crank religion founded by a young speaker. She discovered years later that her publisher, Frank Sheed, had been this young man. Caryll felt that the Guild was what the Catholic Church ought to be—not an institution waiting for the people to come to it, but a community of believers reaching out to people. The Guild was, in a way that she did not realize then, Christ, the Good Shepherd, looking for his lost sheep. He was looking for Caryll.

Emotionally and spiritually empty, Caryll was ripe for an affair. She met a Russian spy, twenty-six years older than she, and fell madly in love. Sidney Reilly was born in Odessa. His father was his mother's doctor and lover, a man named Rosenblum. Sidney appeared in Germany around 1900 as a representative of the firm of Grunberg and Reilly, timber merchants at Port Arthur in southern

Manchuria. They had amassed a fortune from an arms factory and commissions from various German ship-building firms. Somewhere in his travels, he became a naturalized British citizen. His goal as a counterspy was to overthrow the Bolsheviks and make himself the master of Moscow. Caryll undoubtedly met him through her Russian friends, refugees from the revolution. He helped her sell some of her drawings, or at least pretended to do so. Her friends knew he meant far more to her than she did to him. When he made the sudden decision to marry Pepita Chambers in 1923, Caryll was devastated. The loss of his love remained a raw wound for the rest of Caryll's life. Yet because she had loved him, she had been able to love many other people, animals and things, she wrote to a friend in a similar situation.

> The hurt always remains with one—yet no sooner is such a decision really made than one finds those people and experiences that one has been denying coming into one's life like shattering, unimaginable graces—not shattering in a destructive sense, but shattering the walls that any necessarily frustrating experience builds around us when we foster it.
> Maybe while you feel that you have shut the door, you have in reality thrown it open to the true happiness which is really your ultimate good.[3]

Whenever our hopes, our dreams or our inner visions are frustrated, their energy remains locked inside and can cause great turmoil and confusion in our lives. At this point in Caryll's life, energy was blocked on many levels. Her relationships with the people who had been in her life were fractured, her creativity as a writer was hampered by the need to earn a living, her emotional life was shattered by the end of a love affair, her physical life remained fragile and her spiritual life was homeless. It's a wonder that she did not undergo a nervous breakdown. Instead, she experienced an amazing breakthrough—a vision of Christ everywhere and in everyone that lasted for several days and altered the course of her life.

> To surrender all that we are, as we are, to the spirit of love in order that our lives may bear Christ into the world—that is what we shall be asked.[4]

Exercise 5.1. Soulmaking: Times of Searching and Decision

Materials needed: *Pen and journal paper, chairs and pillows conducive to meditation.*

Approximate time: *Forty-five minutes.*

Script for Guide: Just as the seed must die to itself in order to birth the life of the tiny plant, so we must die to the old in order for the new to be born. If we do not do this when we are young, we may remain adolescents for decades, even the rest of our lives. Our spiritual life remains shallow and superficial if we have never questioned the religious truths and practices of our youth. Even if we have been raised in a household that practiced no particular religion, at some point in life we are called to question everything from why we were born to why we have to die. If we cast off this opportunity, we join the cast of the living dead. Caryll described people in this state as those in whom Christ lay dead in the tomb. The crux of the hero's journey is being able to ask the right questions. Caryll went from one spiritual leader to another seeking answers. She read assiduously. Ultimately, she cast all spiritual books aside and began to search for a direct experience of the divine. Although many of her books and letters reflect the traditional teachings of the Catholic Church before the tumultuous changes of Vatican II, she goes far beyond them to insights that came from her inner experiences, especially her struggles with temptation that contrasted so painfully with her deep longing for union with God.

There are some people who seem to have known since they were three years old what they wanted to be: an actor, a piano teacher, a police officer or a doctor. Then there are the rest of us who spend a lifetime trying to discover what it is that we truly want. Careers are only one aspect of our life, however. We are called to much more than the way we make a living or serve others. Dr. Rachel Naomi Remen tells how impressed she was as a little girl when she saw an inscription on a gravestone that read: "Born a human being, died a gastroenterologist." Years later she became a physician herself and realized the tragedy of that statement. We are born not to do something, but to become someone. Until recent times, this was not much of a problem because, for most people, life's unfolding was decided at birth. Women were born to marry, keep house and bear children so that the human race would survive. Men, in most cases, did what their fathers did, and their fathers before them. A person's place in life, in society, was not negotiable. Today, the possibilities our lives may take are legion and we are thrown back upon ourselves to decide what paths to take. We look to others to give us advice and expect God to send us a letter saying, "Do this." The answers, however, lie deep within us. Today we must learn to listen to the voices within and discern which are coming from our true self and which are coming from the ego or false selves. Caryll knew the importance of paying attention to images that welled up from deeper-than-conscious levels of the psyche, for from the beginning she was a poet and a mystic. She explained that her visions were not things she saw outside herself, but things she saw in her "mind's eye."

We are going to practice paying attention to what is happening in our "mind's eye," our inner senses. We begin by entering into an atmosphere of stillness. As we sit in silence, we go inward and focus our attention on the flow of thoughts, images and perceptions that are continually in motion at a level of consciousness we become aware of only in dream states or reverie. Then taking our pen, we record in our journal whatever comes to us, so that it remains accessible to our conscious mind. We do this without judgment, without censoring or editing. If we pick and choose what to record, we have only a partial picture to work with later. When we censor, the partial data that we have gathered gives us a picture that is like a jigsaw puzzle with several pieces missing. So let us put aside censorship and begin.

Seated on the floor or in a chair, we keep our spine erect, allowing our body to relax without slouching. *(Pause)* Closing our eyes, we allow our thoughts to come to rest, our breath to find its own pace. Our stomach rises and falls as we inhale deeply and then exhale, two or three times. Our pen and journal are nearby, ready to record the inner movements of our psyche. As the stillness settles within us, we move back to a time in our life when we came to a fork in the road. We feel once again the tone or mood of that time in our journey. We see, in our mind's eye, a place where we felt comfortable and safe and we go there. In this place, we become aware of the flow of events and circumstances of our life then:

people,
places,
hopes,
dreams,
aspirations,
works in which we were engaged,
beliefs we held,
causes we espoused,
external happenings and inner events,
plans we had and obstacles that stood in the way of
    their fulfillment,
detours,
disappointments,
fears,
decisions we made or failed to make.
And in all of this, we search for the seeds of becoming
that may have been allowed to remain dormant,
but that need to be planted in rich soil,
watered, sunned, and grown to full flowering.
We stop, momentarily, to come back to the surface,
just enough to write or draw what is coming to us from
    the depths of our being,
in the stillness of this silent atmosphere.

Allow about fifteen minutes for writing now. Warn the group when the time is ending: "We have two min-utes left." Bring them back slowly, slowly back to the surface, back into the room, and invite them to open their eyes. Open eyes are one good way to tell when everyone has come back to the surface of consciousness.

Group process: *If the group is open to it, you may invite individuals to read back what they have written. This evokes further awareness that can be added to the entries in their journals.*

Those who wish may simply reread what they have written to themselves and record what happens as they do that. Often this evokes further awareness and entries. A question that may be put to all at this point is, "What aspect of yourself that has lain dormant did you discover? Is this a time in your life when you might choose to allow it to blossom? If so, in what way?"

For those working alone: *Read the script above into a cassette player, then listen to it and record what comes to you in your journal. Pay particular attention to dormant seeds that you might bring to full flowering in your life now.*

Prayer

> Descend,
> Holy Spirit of Life!
> Come down into our hearts,
> that we may live.
> Descend into emptiness,
> that emptiness may be filled.
> Descend into the dust,
> that the dust may flower.
> Descend into the dark,
> that the light
> may shine in darkness.[5]

Chapter 6:
Visions

It is not enough for us, if we live in Christ, to try to imitate what he did, we must also acquire his personality and grow to the maturity of our Christhood through the means by which he grew to his maturity of manhood, so that the trifling things of our experience, transitory by themselves as the fall of a rose, become charged with eternal meanings by the ray of his light.[1]

Caryll's understanding of the indwelling of Christ in everyone evolved through a series of three visions that she recounted in her autobiography, *A Rocking-Horse Catholic*. The first occurred while she was living and studying at a boarding school during the First World War when she was about fourteen. The order of sisters who ran the school was French, so the students were indoctrinated with a fierce hatred of the Germans. One of the lay sisters was Bavarian, and that meant German. She had great difficulty speaking either English or French and seemed to be a lonely woman. One day as Caryll was passing the boot room, she saw this sister sitting alone, cleaning a small pair of shoes that she held in her lap. Caryll wrote:

I stopped and went in, intending to help her to polish the shoes. It was only when I had come quite close to her that I saw that she was weeping; tears were running down her rosy cheeks and falling onto the blue apron and the child's shoes. Abashed, I dropped my eyes and stood in front of her, speechless with embarrassment, completely tongue-tied. I saw her large, toil-worn hands come down onto her lap and fold on the little shoes, and even those hands, red and chapped, with blunted nails, were folding in a way that expressed inconsolable grief.

We were both quite silent, I staring down at her beautiful hands, afraid to look up, not knowing what to say; she weeping soundlessly.

At last, with an effort, I raised my head, and then—I saw—the nun was crowned with the crown of thorns.

I shall not attempt to explain this. I am simply telling the thing as I saw it. That bowed head was weighed under the crown of thorns.

I stood for—I suppose—a few seconds, dumbfounded, and then, finding my tongue, I said to her, "I would not cry, if I was wearing the crown of thorns like you are."

She looked at me as if she were startled, and asked, "What you mean?"

"I don't know," I said, and at the time, I did not.

I sat down beside her, and together we polished the shoes.[2]

The second vision took place while she was working and living at her mother's boarding house in July of 1918. Caryll was on her way to buy some potatoes on a nearby street corner. It was a rainy evening, and as she hurried down the street, she suddenly was held still, as if a magnet held her feet to a particular spot in the middle of the road. In front of her, above her, wiping out every-thing—the gray street, the sky, the whole world—was a gigantic and living Russian icon of Christ the King cruci-fied. She had never seen a Russian icon at the time, but she commented in the recounting of this experience that those she saw later in life never approached the beauty of this vision. It may have lasted only a few minutes, but it seemed like hours. Time became suspended. When she reached the vegetable shop, tears were running down her face. The woman who sold her the potatoes tried to com-fort her, imagining that she was in some kind of trouble. When she could not stop Caryll's tears, she gave her an apple and sent her on her way with the sack of potatoes.

Soon after, perhaps the next day, Caryll saw a placard on the same corner where she had had her vision. It pro-claimed the assassination of the Russian Tsar. Then she understood the meaning of what she had seen, for the face of the Tsar in the newspaper photographs was the face of her Christ the King, but without its glory. From that time on, she was completely dominated by the thought that Russia was the country in which the Pas-sion of Christ was being lived out. She was convinced that her vision and the assassination of the Tsar indi-cated that the conversion of the world to Christ had begun in Russia with the murder of its king. She also realized that Christ was as present in the rich and pow-erful as he was in the poor and oppressed. Her first glimpse of Christ was in the humblest of lay sisters, her second, in a king.

Caryll's third vision broadened her understanding of Christ's indwelling to include every human being. She was on a crowded underground train in London. Workers of every description were jostled together, sitting and straphanging, as they headed home at the end of the day. Suddenly she saw Christ in them all. He was living in them, dying in them, rejoicing in them, sorrowing in them. Because he was in them, and because they were there, the whole world was in that train—not only the world as it was at that moment, but all who had lived in the past and all those yet to come. When she came out into the street, she walked for a very long time through the crowds. The same vision continued. Christ was on every side, in every passerby, everywhere—Christ. This vision lasted with intensity for several days. Caryll saw innumerable implications as she continued to see Christ in everyone, mysteries she pondered for the rest of her life. She realized that Christ had put himself into the hands of sinners, had entrusted himself to us, so that he might be our gift to each other—that we might comfort him in each other and that we might give him to each other. In this way, ordinary life became sacramental, and every action of anyone at all had eternal meaning.

Exercise 6.1. Sharing a Personal Religious Experience

Materials needed: *Chairs in pairs facing each other. Approximate time: One hour.*

Script for Guide: Find a partner. Sit facing each other, close enough to touch each other's fingertips. Then, as you touch fingertips, breathe slowly and deeply in unison for several minutes. *(Pause)* As you sit together, in the silence, remember a time in your life when Christ or some holy person spoke to you of the mysteries of your life. Scripture, the life or writings of a holy person, a dream or a waking vision may lead to an experience of the divine presence in your life. Recall how your experience affected your beliefs, your relationships and your work.

Allow about three minutes for reflection.

Now decide who will go first. One of you is the questioner and the other the responder. I will state a question, and the questioner will repeat it after me. The person answering will have five minutes to reply. Then I will state a second question. The questioner will repeat it and the one answering will have five minutes to reply. After the third question and five minutes for a response, you will trade places. The questioner becomes the one answering, and vice versa. I will repeat the same three questions, allowing five minutes for each answer.

When both persons in each pair have had a turn, I will invite you to ritualize your encounter. This may be done by holding hands and giving each other a blessing, or by other simple gestures of your choice.

1. Tell me, when have you had an experience of the presence of God or of Christ in your life?

2. In what ways have you been called to reflect or manifest the presence of God or Christ to others in your life?

3. How did the experiences you have shared just now alter your life?

Group process: *Share how this experience in pairs went for you. If the group is very large, you may want* *to break into smaller groups. Personal sharing deepens the experience for everyone and may serve to evoke further awareness of God's presence in one's life.*

For those working alone:

1. *Recall a time in your life when you had an experience similar to Caryll's. How were you and the course of your life changed?*

2. *How has a direct encounter with the sacred or the divine affected your faith and what you believe about God?*

3. *Create your own "rhythm" on this theme: sometimes the forces that surround us threaten our inward life, but they are not as strong as the unheard, unseen, unfelt, unimaginably sensitive Christ-life in us that is stronger than the storming, parching, freezing or blighting of any possible environment.*[3] *You may prefer to choose subject matter based upon your own experience.*

Prayer

> Savior of the world,
> take my heart,
> which shrinks
> from the stark realism
> and ugliness of suffering,
> and expand it with Your love.
> Open it wide
> with the fire of Your love,
> as a rose is opened
> by the heat of the sun.
> Lord, take my heart
> and give me yours.[4]

Chapter 7:
Coming Home

For me, the greatest joy in being once again in full communion with the Catholic Church has been, and is now, the ever-growing reassurance given by the doctrine of the Mystical Body of Christ, with its teaching that we are the Church, and that "Christ and His Church are one"—and that because Christ and His Church are one, the world's sorrow, with which I have always been obsessed, and which is a common obsession in these tragic years, is only the shadow cast by the spread arms of the crucified King to shelter us until the morning of resurrection from the blaze of everlasting love.[1]

The sequence of events in Caryll's life is not always clear. What is certain is that her vision of Christ in everyone brought her back to the Roman Catholic Church, for she had a deeply ingrained belief that it was the Mystical Body of Christ. Her visions revealed to her that the Church included everyone, even those she referred to as *unconscious Christs*. It is interesting to note that the Vatican Council's definition of the Church as the People of God did not evolve until a decade after her death.

Caryll lived in a time that sounds much like our own. She wrote in her journal:

> We live in a time that is tortured
> "Between two worlds,
> One dead
> One powerless to be born."

Some people cling to what is past; some, the fewer and braver, face the future; but to live harmoniously in the present is an almost superhuman task.[2] Caryll felt she was living in a time between parentheses. While past ways no longer served, new ways had not come into being. She had no desire, as many Catholics did, either to return to what had been or to make deadening and choking efforts to set "fierce limitations on the uses of the present." She wrote that the most serious duty we have is to see and to recognize Christ in the present moment and to move forward. She believed that looking back to the past is a sin.[3]

Caryll felt more comfortable with the poor and those on the fringes of society than with the privileged in the upper class. She broke her engagement to a wealthy Englishman because he wanted her to learn deportment and to get rid of her accent typical of the western region of England, especially the cities of Bristol and Bath. She wanted to be loved just as she was. Although they did not marry, they remained lifelong friends. His mother, who enjoyed her company, continued to invite her on journeys to other countries. Caryll accompanied her on a trip down the Rhine, but turned down a tour of Australia.

Paradoxically, Caryll lived more than half of her life in the home of a wealthy divorcee. A mutual friend introduced Caryll to Iris Wyndham. Not only did they become fast friends, but when Iris divorced her husband, Richard, she invited Caryll to live with her. Iris obviously accepted Caryll as she was and did not attempt to change her. Many thought that Caryll was taking advantage of Iris' generosity. What they did not know is that Caryll always paid her own expenses. She found it so difficult to ask anyone for financial help that she would go without eating and walk to work if necessary.

Caryll was devoted to Iris and to her daughter Joan. This is apparent in her letters to Joan when she was away on a holiday with Iris. Caryll begged Joan not to jump on her mother whom she described as fragile; to make sure she ate a lot of bread, cream and sweets; and not to let her get too tired.

When Caryll first moved in with Iris, Caryll's mother Gert "cast gloom," a state anyone who knew her dreaded. However, within the next few years, Caryll and her mother were reconciled. Gert accompanied Iris on a weekend at a famous country house disguised as her maid. Dressed in a neat black dress and stockings, she carried out the part perfectly, but complained that since Iris had no title, she had been seated at the bottom of the table in the servant's hall. Caryll and Iris also paid visits to her father Wilmott on his yacht from time to time.

During this period, a friend of Caryll's who had spent some time in the convent asked her why she hadn't become a nun. Caryll's answer was that no convent would accept her. Whether that was true or not, Caryll chose the single life. Maisie Ward comments that Caryll was convinced that her vocation was not for herself alone, but for others.[4] In this, Caryll modeled her belief that all people are called to holiness, not just those who are set apart in monasteries, rectories, and convents. Caryll drew people to Christ by continuing to live in the fashionable society of Iris' family and the bohemian world of the artists who were her friends.

Caryll brought several of her friends into the church, including Iris. Father Geoffrey Bliss, S.J., her spiritual director, asked her to write articles and illustrate them for *The Messenger of the Sacred Heart* and *The Children's Messenger.* She also became a friend of the founder of the Grail Society, Baroness Yvonne Bosch van Drakestein, who had come to England from Holland in 1932. She helped with Grail displays and with their magazine. One of her best sets of the Stations of the Cross was made for their chapel. But she soon came to realize that the Grail, like most movements that become institutionalized, was more interested in organizing for a *visible* kingdom on earth than in nurturing the Christ-life in people's souls. This could be observed in the tendency of members to attract people who were like themselves. Caryll criticized their attempts to bring about unity by shaping people who were different into an unnatural conformity. She had experienced this in her boarding school days when the sisters emphasized the ideal of the "Catholic lady." This ideal was based more on external comportment than on the development of an inner life and one's individuality.

Caryll was ahead of her time in valuing diversity. Today we have become more aware of the great diversity in nature itself and the richness that complexity brings to life. Caryll wrote that we must "come to understand the great diversity of being that needs must be if the community is to come to the full flower and fruit of the fullness of Christhood."[5]

Exercise 7.1 Dialogue

Materials needed: *Paper and pen.*
Approximate time: *Forty-five minutes to one hour.*
Script for Guide: One of Caryll's practices during this period of her life was to write dialogues. This method enabled Caryll to explore more than one point of view. One of the topics she explored was the creation of idols, false images of God and of Christ. These images were nothing more than projections of our own egos. Caryll understood that our conception of God can be like that of the jealous husband who demands that we give up all human love because it competes with rather than completes love of the divinity. We can create a God who is waiting to catch us in some little offense and who is in a continual state of being aggrieved with us. Or we can create a convenient God who winks at the flagrant flaunting of our lust for wealth, fame and power.

Caryll was known to sit up half the night discussing religion with her friends. In the 1930s and 1940s, these were more than likely to be intellectual debates. Her dialogues looked something like this:

A. You need to respect the rights of others and at the same time be able to hold fast to your own integrity. You should have a sufficient knowledge of your faith to enable you to explain it when called upon.

B. I think example is most important. Arguing turns people off.

A. Off what?

B. God.

A. No, only stupid arguing turns people off. Instead of letting people discover what God is really like, you tell them your own ideas. You want them to be attracted to you and how much you know, not to God.

B. Well, you Catholics worship statues!

A. No, we don't. We pray to the saints they represent. You, on the other hand, worship false gods such as money, respectability and health.

B. I disagree. Wealth, respect and health are gifts God gives to us. God put gold in the earth because he meant for us to use it. Only a fool seeks to be laughed at, and we have a duty to protect our health.

A. Well, I believe those three lead us to more pernicious idols.

B. I can hardly imagine what they might be!

We can tap into our own deep, inner wisdom through the writing of dialogue scripts. A dialogue requires that we enter into the mutual meeting of two persons. In her dialogue, Caryll had to enter into the mind of each person and speak from each one's point of view. She did not indicate that either one represented herself. The ability to see reality from another's point of view as well as our own enables us to participate in a unifying field that leads to integrity, to wholeness and to truth. In this exercise, we are going to enter into a dialogue with another person whom we consider to have great wisdom. It may be someone who is or has been our mentor such as an aunt, an uncle or a grandparent. It may be a great historical figure, a saint or Jesus. Take some time now to choose someone with whom you would like to enter into dialogue in this present moment.

Has each of you chosen a wisdom figure? I want to warn you that regardless of whom you may have chosen, somebody else may appear when you move into a deeper place within yourself. Whoever shows up is the one with whom you need to dialogue right now, so don't be surprised. Have your paper and pen handy to record what is said; then close your eyes and relax. For a few minutes, focus your attention on your breath. Do not try to breathe in any particular way; just allow your breath to find its own pace.

(Pause)

Continuing to relax your body, letting go of any tension you may be aware of, allow the breath to become slow, your thoughts to come to rest. You are still, like water that has become calm, like a pond with no ripples. Sitting quietly, spine erect, not thinking about anything in particular, you find yourself in a place that is sacred to you, a place where you feel safe and comfortable. In this holy place, a person appears to you, a wise being. You may not see this person; you may simply hear a voice or feel a presence. You greet this person. He or she responds. And the dialogue begins. You may ask questions, issues that have been burning in your heart for a long time. You listen to the answers and record what is said. You speak, your wisdom figure replies, and the dialogue continues as long as necessary. You speak, your wisdom figure speaks, and you record what is said in the quiet atmosphere of this sacred place.

Allow at least twenty minutes for recording. Warn the group when two or three minutes remain.

81

Now it is time to say good-bye to your wisdom figure. Ask for a blessing, a word of comfort, encouragement or admonition from your wisdom figure. Then thank that person, and when you are ready return slowly to this room, continuing to record what is coming to you in your journal. You may want to reread what you have recorded, paying particular attention to what stirs in you as you do so and adding your new awareness as an additional entry at the end of your dialogue.

Group process: *Invite those who so wish to read their dialogue script aloud. After each reading, invite the reader to reflect upon what stirred inside as he or she read and to record that awareness as a footnote to the dialogue.*

For those working alone: *Record the script leading into the dialogue on a cassette recorder. Then listen to it and enter into the experience of writing your own inner wisdom dialogue script.*

Pay particular attention to what emotions, thoughts, memories, and other forms of awareness stir in you as you write and as you reread to yourself later what you have recorded.

Prayer

Into Your hands, O Lord,
into Your hands
we commit our living and dying,
knowing
that You are
the dawn of eternal day,
the burning light of the morning star.[6]

Chapter 8:
Sprats

Love is most likely to spring from another's need of us, and the fact of spending ourselves for another always generates new life in us. To give life is the purpose of love, and we love those people most of all whose needs waken a response in us that floods us with creative energy, causing us to put out new green shoots of life.[1]

Caryll's involvement with both the rich and the poor enabled her to network, to be a bridge, so to speak, between them. Living with Iris gave Caryll the freedom to find her place in the world and to express herself artistically, not only through woodcarving and creating images with words, but also on the level of social service. In the 1930s Caryll had a secure job at Grosse's, a business dedicated to the decoration of churches, but she was tormented by the troubles of others. One day, Caryll and two of the partners of Grosse's, Louis Billaux and Jacques Doneux, along with two girls on the staff, were discussing the story of the multiplication of the loaves and the fishes. Noting what Jesus had done with five loaves of bread and two fish, Caryll suggested that each of them put down a penny for the poor. She said that if

God wanted them to do something for the poor, God would multiply the coins. Just then the father of Louis, Charles Billaux, came into the room, looked with puzzlement at the coins, and said, "Whatever those are for, I will multiply them." He laid down five shillings.

This happy omen led that group to found a small society called "The Loaves and Fishes." There were five members already, the loaves, and two new members comprised the fishes. Working members were known as "Sprats," and the chairperson, whose identity was kept secret, was the Red Herring. Those who received help from the organization were known as "sea horses." They were the "unofficial poor" who fell through the cracks of the welfare system: the unskilled, the unemployed, the sick, the old who had never earned enough to save for their retirement and the young who had no family to help them. Aid was given discreetly. The names of those being helped were divulged only when absolutely necessary. Each sprat tried to catch a mackerel, a rich person who was willing to give a single donation, large or small. Worthiness was not a criteria for receiving help; it was given according to need. At the end of one year, there were ninety-eight sprats. Money went to a woman with pyorrhea for false teeth, because her bad breath had kept her from getting a job. Home help was provided for a distraught woman whose baby needed constant nursing. Employment was found for those out of work. This organization continued long after Caryll's death.

One of Caryll's poems, "Philip Speaks," was inspired by the work of the Sprats:

The Lord blessed the bread.
He put it into our hands
and it multiplied,
not in *His* hands but in *mine!*[2]

Caryll was a social artist, a person who was full of ideas for meeting the needs of others.[3] She said she was one to plant the seed. Others had to carry the project to fruition. Caryll was able to treat all people with respect, regardless of what they had done or how they looked. She saw their true potential, the Christ lying hidden within. She was able to make people laugh, shaking them loose from old ways of thinking and being. She was able to face the dark side of life as well as the bright and to attack problems head on. She did not mince words. She was able to say to people struggling with temptation, "I can tell you what the right thing to do is objectively, but if I were in your situation, I don't think I could be as strong or courageous as you are." She was full of new ideas, ways to bring about a more just society in the years immediately after World War II. Many of these ideas remained in the realm of her imagination: a Catholic bookstore in the heart of London where people could offer poetry readings, listen to good recorded classical music, review and discuss the latest books; and a home for women convicted of murder once they were released from prison. Caryll hoped to provide a home for children with her friend Charles Scott-Paton as administrator and Iris Wyndham as the cook.

One project that Caryll did not think of herself was suggested by Monsignor Ronald Knox, a Roman Catholic priest who had written many spiritual books and a new translation of the Bible in contemporary English. He sent the only fan letter in his life to Caryll urging her to open a school of spirituality for the writers of devotional books.

Writing was the path that Caryll chose to devote herself to in the end. She felt that she could reach more people this way than in any other, and that conviction has proven to be true. Her books have inspired unknown numbers of people. The breadth and depth of her impact has been and continues to be immeasurable.

Exercise 8.1 Becoming a Foster Parent of the Divine Child

Materials needed: *Circles of chairs for small groups, six to eight in number.*

Approximate time: *Forty-five minutes.*

Script for Guide: Caryll wrote often about the Divine Child in us. This Child took upon himself the sorrows of the world and, in doing so, redeemed them. We are called, first of all, to recognize this Child in our own being, especially the child who has been forced to flee his own country and live among strangers in an alien land. Then we need to become foster parents to what she called the "Divine Foundling." This can be any person who shares some of the essential characteristics of childhood: dependence, poverty and the necessity to obey. This may be someone who is very old or an invalid, someone who is unstable or borderline, someone in prison, someone who has been institutionalized, someone who is a delinquent, someone who is homeless or someone who is a refugee. In the past century, we have tended to delegate responsibility for these people to charitable organizations and the government. Their care has become the responsibility of social workers, hospitals, food pantries and shelters. The increasing neediness of more and more people in the world overwhelms us. We blame the welfare system for creating an underclass of people who are dependent on handouts and are unable to work because they are illiterate and unskilled. The government, no longer able to finance the care of so many, attempts to return responsibility back to the private sector, especially the churches, mosques and synagogues. This cycle of blame and government cutbacks contains no simple answer.

In small groups of six or eight people, search your own hearts for the part God is calling you to play, large or small, both as the Divine Child who has been lost or forced to flee and as a foster parent of the Divine Foundling. Take five or ten minutes in silence to reflect before you begin to share.

For those working alone: *Take as much time as necessary to reflect upon your experience as a lost child or refugee. Then listen to how God is calling you to become the foster parent of that lost or exiled child. Record your reflections in your journal.*

Prayer

Give us,
most humble Savior,
the humility to forget ourselves
and even our sinfulness,
so that we may never allow consciousness of our
own unworthiness
to prevent us from helping You
in any man
whom we meet on the way
in need.[4]

Chapter 9:
War and the Passion
of Christ

Experience has taught us that war simplifies life.
Every individual would experience some equiva-
lent of the Passion even if there were no war; but
war makes it visible and even simple, and shows us
how the Passion of Christ can be each one's indi-
vidual secret and at the same time something
shared by the whole world.[1]

From 1939 until 1944, Caryll devoted herself to the
war effort. First aid work involved working in gas
decontamination three twelve-hour shifts a week, some
during the day, others at night. She was alarmed at the
degree of sheer physical energy coping with such work
required. Her lungs were sore from being in gas-proof
rooms wearing a gas mask. According to Maisie Ward,

> Caryll was terrified during the raids. Instead of kid-
> ding herself by trying to minimize the danger, she
> said to herself, "For as long as this raid lasts—an
> hour—or eight hours—you are going to be terrified.
> So are lots of people who don't deserve it as you do,
> so you must carry on and be terrified, that's all."[2]

Caryll's sense of humor, not obvious in her writing, kept her friends and herself going during difficult times. One time she did a ludicrous dance while the bombs were falling. A friend, Dickie, said she looked like a clown or a puppet whose bones are loose in the sockets, a tragicomedy of a high order. Iris described her as a stringed puppet that made faces so ghastly people couldn't help giggling. During first aid training, Caryll was supervised by a starched and stiff head nurse who called people by their family names. As Caryll was scrubbing up in preparation for a dressing, the head nurse asked, "Houselander, are you sterile?" Caryll could not help answering, "Not as far as I know."

Caryll could not understand how the human race could be dragged into the violence of war. Then in a blinding flash of understanding she saw that Christ had not resisted evil; in fact he had allowed himself to be put to death violently. From then on, she understood that war is a participation in the passion of Christ. Although the reality of war in the world remained incomprehensible, Caryll noted that the evils she was seeing in this war had always existed: fear, hunger, destitution, disease, frustration and death. The only difference this time was that these evils were more out in the open.[3] She remained in London during the entire Blitz, sometimes fire-watching on roofs, sometimes helping in the hospital, and at other times serving in the Mobile First Aid unit on the street. In 1941, she began working in the Censorship Office. She became aware of the wounds, anxieties, courage and simple joys of the people of the world as she checked the parcels and prayed for everyone connected with them.

The Spiritual Path of Caryll Houselander

Caryll published *This War Is the Passion* in 1941. She wrote that the enemies assailing Christianity were not only the dark forces apparent to all, but also the subtle temptations that a prosperous world never ceases to propose to individual Christians and the gradual loss of the sharp edge of the uncompromising simplicity of Christ's love. Believing that through love alone we would be saved from being swept away by hate, fear and despair, she did not dwell on the cruelty of war. It was etched forever in the memories of those who experienced its brutality. Caryll wrote that the mystery of war couldn't be understood by our minds; it can only be experienced by our hearts. In this sense, war takes on meaning only when understood in the light of the mystery of the passion and death of Jesus Christ. Caryll understood that the merit of our own sufferings and sacrifices was not dependent upon how distasteful they were. Caryll's explanation of sacrifice had to do with giving one's complete attention and placing one's whole concentration on God. For a child, making the Sign of the Cross was this kind of sacrifice, because for that moment, the child had turned itself totally toward God.

When we lose the awareness of God in our lives, we adore anything that assumes mystery because it is bigger than we are. The adoration of false gods, whether they are the machine or the state, is what leads to international conflict. The crisis of war offers the opportunity to participate in the passion of Christ. It is the bridge to God calling us to contemplation. This contemplation leads us to identify with Christ, to become one with him, to love others with his love, to look at them with his eyes, and to comfort them with his hands. The height of this identification is coming to love even our enemies and to be able to forgive them with his heart, the way he had done on the cross when he said, "Father, forgive them, for they do not know what they do" (Luke 23:34).

Caryll was not as deluded as those who believed that after the war everyone would be kinder, wiser and more just, and that social conditions would improve as a result. She knew that the aftermath of the war would outlast the natural lifetime of anyone living then, and that bitterness, poverty, disillusionment and despair were just as likely to occur as would a bright future. Nevertheless, she did believe Christ would rise again, not by any mass revival movement, but secretly in the human heart through the power of the Holy Spirit who teaches all wisdom, gives vision and strength, comforts and renews.

Exercise 9.1 A Time for Reflection

Materials needed: *Circles of five or six chairs.*
Approximate time: *Forty-five minutes.*
Script for Guide: Discuss in small groups how you see Christ's passion continuing in the world today. One of the most heinous crimes of World War II was the extermination of millions of people in the Holocaust. Many wonder how the German people could know what was going on and look the other way. Think about ways in which other "holocausts" continue in the world today. Who is looking away now? Why don't we rise up and protest the horrors going on in our own country and around the world?

Group process: *Report back to the entire group the insights gained in your small group discussions.*

For those working alone. *Make a list of all the ways you are aware of the continuing passion of Christ in the world today. For one month search the newspapers, magazines, and Internet for examples of suffering in the world.*

Exercise 9.2 The Way of the Cross— A Modern Mystery Play

Materials needed: *Props and costumes*

Approximate time: *Two hours and thirty minutes.*

Script for Guide: Caryll wrote and performed in many plays with her mother and friends. The scripts seem to have been lost, but her friend Iris recalled one in particular where Caryll and her mother performed in "Aladdin and the Lamp." In a letter to Archie Campbell-Murdoch, a friend who ran a school for boys, she suggested he keep up the acting tradition by forming a school company of mystery players along medieval lines. Then she wrote something startling. She recommended that they put together a repertoire of simple little mystery plays and go to villages where there were no priests. They were to act them in the open air. If funds allowed they might hire (even borrow) a local wagon for a stage and bring some light and simple props. "I am sure the time has come when the evangelizing of the countryside will be the great apostolate. Is it not the right moment to bring the Mass back to all the little villages? I think your mystery players would be a very real apostolate."[4]

Passion plays that reenact the suffering and death of Jesus continue to our present time. In Roman Catholicism, a longstanding tradition has been the Way of the Cross. Caryll wrote and illustrated her own version of the Stations published by Sheed & Ward in 1955. She pointed out that the fourteen Stations of the Cross enable us to connect our own individual stories with the passion of Christ and the stories of suffering in the world. She wrote, "The Stations show us how each one can lighten the heavy cross that is laid upon the bent back of the whole human race, how each one in the power of Christ's love can sweeten his own suffering and that of those who are dear to him."[5]

The tender, rhythmic prayer of the Way of the Cross has been repeated on millions of lips over the ages. Caryll writes,

> How dark it is,
> how heavy and sweet!
> How wide the wound
> in the broken heart!
> How fast the nails
> in the hands and feet.[6]

The traditional stations of the Way of the Cross retell the story of Jesus' suffering from his sentencing by Pontius Pilate to the placement of his dead body in the tomb. More recent versions add a fifteenth station: the Resurrection. Some of the stations are legendary rather than biblical in nature.

1. Jesus Is Condemned to Death.
2. Jesus Receives His Cross.

3. Jesus Falls for the First Time.
4. Jesus Meets His Mother.
5. Simon Helps Jesus To Carry the Cross
6. Veronica Wipes the Face of Jesus.
7. Jesus Falls the Second Time.
8. Jesus Speaks to the Women of Jerusalem.
9. Jesus Falls the Third Time.
10. Jesus Is Stripped of His Garments.
11. Jesus Is Nailed to the Cross
12. Jesus Dies on the Cross.
13. Jesus Is Taken Down from the Cross.
14. Jesus Is Laid in the Tomb.

Depending on the number of participants, divide into enough groups to allow each to take one Station. If there are a small number of people, each group may need to take two or three Stations. For each Station of the Cross, create a current situation that parallels the experience of Jesus. For example, portray a person who has been condemned to death unjustly, or dramatize a woman holding her dead son in her arms. Each presentation should be limited to a maximum of five minutes. Allow one hour for the groups to prepare their script and to find props and costumes.

Group process: *After the dramatic enactments have been completed, spend at least fifteen minutes in the large group processing the experiences of both actors and audience.*

For those working alone. *Create your own contemporary Way of the Cross with pictures taken from magazines and newspapers for each station.*

Prayer

Christ, grant us, when all seems lost, when there seems no hope any more, to acknowledge our God, Who is our hope, Who is All that is. In Your Name we believe in God: "Though He should slay me, yet will I trust in Him."[7]

> Into Your hands, O Lord,
> into Your hands
> we commit our living and dying,
> knowing
> that You are
> the dawn of eternal day,
> the burning light of the morning star.[8]

Chapter 10:
Caryllinati—
Caryll's Wisdom School

Christ is among us
His heart like a rose
expanding within us....[1]

Caryll's friends called their group *Caryllinati*. They were inspired by the practice of St. Catherine of Siena's followers who were known as *Caterinati*. One of the *Caryllinati* was Christine Spender, sister of the poet Stephen. During the war she worked with Caryll in the Censorship Office. Christine was startled the first time she saw Caryll, thinking she must have come straight from an artist's studio, or that perhaps she was an actress. Caryll's flaming red hair was cut in a pageboy style that hung nearly to her shoulders. Despite the protests of all her friends, she whitened her face with a powder that gave her a ghoulish appearance. Her very thick glasses added to the curious dignity and gravity with which she carried herself. Although some might have described her as quaint, Christine thought she might just as well have stepped out of a medieval stained-glass window. An invisible arc of light seemed to shine on her.[2] In her letters

96

to Christine after the war, Caryll mentioned that she was self-conscious about her looks—not only her looks, but also her very presence. She said she felt her soul was even worse than her body and that every personal revelation became an added indecency.[3]

Caryll wanted to write more than she wanted to live. This passion transported her beyond self-criticism and self-consciousness. The articles, books and poems she felt driven to write taught her an amazing number of things she had no idea of when she picked up her pen. A profound wisdom seemed to bubble up from her depths. While listening to people for hours every day drained her, Caryll noted that writing renewed her energy. She knew from experience that if she did not express herself through creative work, the energy did not go into some other activity but flickered out altogether. She commented that when creative artists are frustrated for several months, they cease to have any energy at all. It was this fact that led her to encourage Christine to begin to write and to stop letting her brother's fame get in the way.

Another member of the *Caryllinati* was Archie Campbell-Murdoch. At the beginning of the war he had offered her sanctuary in his flat because she had a great deal of trouble getting any writing done. Constantly besieged by people knocking at her door, she may have been describing herself when she wrote in *Guilt,*

> There are those who must live, as it were, in other men's hands; whose success, even if it be of a spiritual order, must be paid for in a suffering of poverty far more terrible than material poverty, a poverty of not having themselves, not having anything of their

own—not time, or solitude, or their thoughts, or
even their senses: their hearing filled always with
other men's troubles, their eyes with the face of
other people's sorrow, all their words given to
others without stint for their comfort, their touch
the perpetual touch of healing and blessing.[4]

Caryll was accessible to everyone who came to her
for help. One friend felt worse after unburdening herself
to Caryll, rather than better, because Caryll was so
empathic. Caryll took the sufferings of others upon herself, which explains why she suffered so much from
fatigue and even from physical illness. Caryll's physician claimed that Caryll was not neurotic, but that she
was extremely sensitive. It was this sensitivity that
enabled her to help and understand people but also
made her extremely vulnerable.

After the war, Caryll went one day a week for a
period that lasted over two years to Archie's school at
Frensham for boys who had been traumatized by war.
This required leaving London early in the morning,
teaching all day and returning home late at night. She
did arts and crafts with them and engaged many of her
friends in providing materials for their projects. Her
imaginative flair led her to teach drawing by inviting the
boys to picture themselves in their mind's eye as cave-
men. They drew messages on the wall of a cave (represented by brown paper) with white and red chalk and
charcoal. She wanted them to learn that art is first of all
saying something. Later they made a crib and figures for
Christmas. During Lent they studied the Last Supper,
making a portable altar, painting a crucifix and carving
simple wooden candlesticks. Her interdisciplinary

approach included reading the scriptures aloud, writing down everything Jesus and the disciples might have used, relating the Last Supper and the passion to the celebration of the Eucharist, and listening to sacred music. She created clubs according to the structure of medieval guilds with a period of probation to judge the quality of work, care of tools and cooperative spirit. Everything she did was aimed at nurturing the life of Christ in these boys who probably suffered from what is known today as post-traumatic stress syndrome. One boy had driven a tank, another had lived alone in the Malayan jungle after the murder of his parents, while others had been held back in life by fearful or over-protective mothers.

Dr. Eric Strauss, a well-known and respected neurologist and psychiatrist, sent emotionally disturbed boys to Caryll. In an era when art and music were not considered therapeutic and the suggestion that they might be a source of healing was rejected, Caryll engaged in art projects with these boys and they recovered. She considered Dr. Strauss to be a genius in his ability to see how art and music can be and must be used as an expression of love that leads to healing.

Dr. Strauss referred to Caryll as that "divine eccentric." In a conversation with Maisie Ward, he asked if she thought Caryll had mystical experiences. He answered his own question by pointing out her unusual insight and perception, even outside the religious sphere. He went on to discuss the relationship between religious visions and psychic phenomena, and the borderline between the two. Caryll had had such amazing results with the boys that Dr. Strauss began to send adult patients to her for "social therapy." Maisie asked him if Caryll had had any training for this. He replied that she did not, but that she had a natural genius. "What exactly is 'social therapy'?" Maisie asked, confessing her ignorance. He answered that in Caryll's case it meant she loved them back to life.[5]

Part of her success was undoubtedly due to the fact that Caryll considered herself as broken and wounded as those who came to her for help. She did not approach them as if she were an expert mechanic and they were a machine with malfunctioning parts that needed to be fixed. She was able to be one with them. By entering into their suffering, she knew just what they needed to become whole. She also saw the potential that lay hidden within them and drew it out. She wrote to a friend, Henry Tayler, about her first client:

> I am able to put into practice all my theories about psychology, and I have great hope that from our poor little shed and this one strange lovely boy, our wisdom school may really begin. Pedro has a mind like a beautiful valley almost hidden by a dark and shadowy twilight. In that twilight one hears the sound of tears and yet finds rare and isolated flowers growing, and these flowers have a positively sparkling brilliance.[6]

The shed she refers to was located in the garden at Milborne Grove where Caryll and Iris lived beginning about 1935. Caryll used it as a workshop for carving wood. It consisted of two chairs, a table, a bench at which she carved and an oil stove for the winter months.

In another letter to Henry she explained that we can't help children if we don't suffer with them. She gave all her spare time to the boys, sharing their sense of defeat and shame and walking with them step by step through dark valleys in order to bring them out again into the light. One thing she did not do was to make them dependent upon her. She thought it a thousand times more vital to help them find their own integrity, stand on their own feet, and leave her. Her own humility shines through her statement, "They are most exacting and demand *everything* one has, but guilelessly. I think we can never understand little children. We can only serve them on our knees."[7]

Caryll poured all her personal experience and her work of being an instrument in the healing of others into her book, *Guilt*. In it she proposed that the great repression of our time was not sex, as Freud believed, but the repression of Christ in the self. The beginning of integrity was to open one's heart to the love of God. Her experience at Frensham and with Dr. Strauss' patients convinced Caryll that parents frustrated their children by failing to see Christ in them. They reduced their children to mediocrity by robbing them of the wonder and mystery that are their right and their necessity. Instead of reading fairy stories and fables in which Christ was always the hero in disguise, they took courses that would prepare them for some dull profession. Good social standing and earning as much money as possible were the only goals most parents set for their children.

Caryll obviously favored Carl Jung's psychology, not Freud's. She was particularly interested in the forces called *archetypes,* which break into consciousness from our depths in the form of symbols, dreams, fantasy, art and poetry, and worldwide myths and fairy stories. In Caryll's mind Christ was the great archetypal pattern

101

for every human being. She cited examples of this pattern from experiences in the life of Jesus and compared them to human experience across the ages. She understood that Jesus, the Light of the World, was the incarnation of the second person of the Holy Trinity who existed from all eternity. She wrote,

> We go through life with dark forces within us and around us, haunted by the ghosts of repudiated terrors and embarrassments, assailed by devils, but we are also continually guided by invisible hands; our darkness is lit by many little flames, from night-lights to the stars. Those who are afraid to look into their own hearts know nothing of the light that shines in the darkness.[8]

Caryll was half a century ahead of those writing today about the re-enchantment of just about every aspect of life. She wrote that we live in a world of disenchantment. The cure is to recapture the essential qualities of childhood: to live in the eternal now, to see the invisible in the visible, to touch the intangible in the tangible, to live in the world of the wonder and mystery of nature and the magic of myth. We are to keep the poet alive in ourselves and say with Christ, "See, I make all things new" (Rev 21:5). We are to live with the constant awareness of the gifts God has strewn at our feet. We are all called to be children of God and to radiate Christ.

Caryll was also decades ahead of those promoting creation spirituality. She deplored the plight of the worker who had become nothing more than a cog in a machine. She believed that we are all born to be co-makers with God. She asserted that work is not just drudgery we have to endure to earn money to survive. It is a participation in cocreation with God. Maisie Ward commented that Caryll did not understand that few people are able to support themselves being artists. However, Caryll must have been aware of this from her own experience of poverty. Caryll's point was that whatever we do, we must keep the artist's *ideal* always before us, and that is to do it with love, not just to earn money. She wrote in *The Risen Christ* that the ideal artist embodies the image of the Blessed Trinity. Artists fashion from some substance outside of themselves that which is in their hearts. When they take their work into their hands and look at it, they see the image and likeness of their inmost, invisible selves.[9]

Caryll included everyone in this idea of the creation of a work of art. She did not intend that we should get around the dilemma of meaningless work by finding a spare-time hobby such as baking whole grain bread, weaving our own clothes that hang like "bags of sackcloth," or throwing our own pots on a potter's wheel. Everyone from the company director to children doing their lessons at school was to become "another Christ," participating in the joy of the creator and undoing the false concept that work is a punishment for sin.

Exercise 10.1 Guilt

Materials needed: *Pen and paper.*
Approximate time: *Thirty minutes.*
Script for Guide: Dr. Karl Menninger wrote that the psychiatric profession had done humanity a great disservice by taking away the sense of guilt and the need for repentance.[10] He said that there are times when we

need to feel guilty about something we have done or have failed to do, and that it is healthy to accept responsibility, confess to someone and ask forgiveness. Caryll was not concerned about this kind of guilt, however, She wrote about two other aspects of guilt: feeling guilty when we haven't done anything wrong and not feeling guilty when we have. In her book, *Guilt,* she included case histories ranging from canonized saints to mass murderers. She cited examples of people who committed cold-blooded murder and were more upset that their clothes were soiled by the spattering of blood than they were about the fact they had just taken another person's life. Then there were those who confessed to crimes they didn't commit. The saints, of course, fell somewhere between those two extremes. Aware of the immense mercy and goodness of God, they felt great remorse at the slightest offense.

It might be helpful to distinguish guilt from shame. Guilt is a conscious awareness of having broken a moral or penal code. Shame, on the other hand, is a feeling of being flawed or diminished and never being able to measure up to what one thinks one should be. Shame is the result of humiliation, of being put down, of coming from a family that is very poor or dysfunctional. This manifests itself in a lowering of one's sense of self-worth. Shame brings a chronic pain that does not go away. This may have been the case early in Caryll's life when she realized that confessing sins did not take away her anxiety, that her very being needed to be transformed.

Take about fifteen minutes now to write about your own experience of guilt. Describe times when you have felt guilty. Was your guilt justified or not? Have you ever done something that you ought to have felt guilty about but didn't? How have you dealt with your guilt feelings (stuffed them, gone to confession, told a close friend, told an absolute stranger you thought you'd never see again, blamed someone or something else)?

Group process: *Find a partner. Share whatever you feel comfortable about revealing your experiences of guilt. You do not have to tell the details. Speak of how you felt as you were reflecting and writing, and talk about guilt in your life. You might want to say something about the experience of remembering times when you felt guilty. Decide who will speak first and who will listen. Those who are the listeners, be attentive and say little. Practice being a compassionate ear who accepts the other person with unconditional love. After each person has had a chance to speak, return to the large group and process your experience.*

For those working alone: *Write about your experiences of guilt. Read what you have written and pay close attention to what thoughts, memories and emotions are evoked as you do so. Record what comes to you as an additional entry in your journal.*

Exercise 10.2 The Way of Expressive Art

Materials needed: *Pencils, pens, colored pencils or crayons, large sheets of art paper and lined loose-leaf paper.*

Approximate time: *Thirty to forty-five minutes.*

Script for Guide: Take a pencil or pen and with your nondominant hand draw a single, continuous random line around a large sheet of blank paper. It may wind and spiral, but it must not be broken. When you are finished drawing the line, put down your pen and stare at the page with soft eyes until an image emerges. Then fill in the image with various colors.

When your image is complete, take a sheet of loose-leaf paper or your journal and list the steps that occurred in the creation of your image. For example, "I began when (Ann) drew a random line on a sheet of art paper with her nondominant hand." Speak in the first person as if you were the image. Continue to use the first person throughout your description. What happened next? "Ann stared at the drawing for a long time." And then what? Proceed until you reach a point where the image has completed the story of its creation. Keep your pen and paper handy.

I am going to lead you into a dialogue with the image you have created as if it were a person. So having your pen and pencil handy to record, sit in a comfortable position, spine erect, close your eyes and relax. Remember to breathe deeply. Moving into a place somewhere between being fully awake and completely asleep, drift back to the room where you slept as a child. You are in the room now. Somewhere under the eaves, there is a closet. You move into it. Pushing aside the clothes hanging there you find a little door on the back wall. You open it and discover a cold, gray, stone staircase that winds down into the darkness. You begin to descend. Feel your way carefully step by step. As you approach the bottom of the stairs, there is a faint light. You are in a large underground room. Its walls are full of ancient symbols. You see another door and open it. Outside this room you find a pier. A small boat is tied to it. You get into the boat, release the rope connecting it to the pier, and begin to drift downstream. The water laps gently on the sides of the boat, lulling you into a dreamlike state. Feeling sleepy, you lie down on the bottom of the boat. It continues to float gently downstream until you come to a grassy shoreline. You pull the boat onshore and begin to explore this place. Suddenly an image appears before you. You recognize it immediately and invite it to join you on the soft green grass. You speak and the image answers. You feel drawn to ask it who or what it is. It speaks to you of the key events of your life. Feeling more comfortable and trusting now, you ask it questions that have been haunting you—questions about your past and things you wonder about your future. The image responds, making clear to you certain patterns in your life, patterns both personal and universal. *(Pause)*

Now it is time to say good-bye to your image and to depart. You say your farewells as you head toward your little boat. You get in and find yourself floating back upstream. As you do, you reflect on the meeting you have had with your image. *(Pause)* Your boat bumps gently into the pier. You grab the rope and tie it securely before getting out. Then, finding the door to the underground room, you start up the stairs. They are lighted now and you have no trouble ascending them. At the top, you crawl through the little door to the closet and return to your childhood bedroom. When you are ready, move slowly, slowly, back to the present moment and to this room and open your eyes.

Group Process: *Take some time now to record your dialogue. Reflect upon how you felt, what emotions* *were evoked, what you discovered about yourself, and how you feel right now. Do you have a sense of being connected to larger-than-personal patterns in your life? Do they resemble any fairy tale or myth? What did you learn about your past? What intimations did you receive about your future? Share your reflections with one other person in the room.*

For those working alone: *Record the guided meditation in Exercise 10.2 on a cassette tape and listen to it in a quiet place. Taking the same questions as those for the Group Process, record your thoughts and feelings in your journal.*

Prayer

> Lord,
> give us the wisdom
> that knows there is no sanctity
> except in love
> and the living of love.[11]

Chapter 11:
Rhythms

*Prayer alone can teach us to concentrate again,
can lead us to absolute trust in God, and make our
minds ready for other essential things...for the
contemplation (not mere observation) of beauty.*[1]

Caryll addressed these words to people living in the
midst of war. Much had been provided to protect them
physically, but nothing had been done to build defenses
for the mind against fear, lack of privacy, loss of individuality, physical shock and nervous tension. She noted
that shock made it very hard to think and even more
difficult to concentrate. Being uprooted from one's regular routines also affected the ability to be focused.

The first defense was to pray all the time and everywhere. Caryll introduced ordinary people to the ancient
methods that had been practiced by Buddhists, Jews,
Muslims, Russian pilgrims and Christians for millennia.
For Buddhists, it meant being mindful. For Jewish mys-
tics, it meant becoming fully present, empty and
focused. For the Russian pilgrim, it meant repeating the
prayer "Lord Jesus, have mercy on me" continually. For
the writer of *The Cloud of Unknowing,* it meant saying
short prayers, single words such as "Help!" that pierced

heaven. St. Ignatius proposed contemplating a single word until all of its meaning had been savored. Undoubtedly Caryll was familiar with all of these. She added to them one that she found helped her open her whole being to God as well as sustain an inner harmony and balance in spite of the shattering and disturbing things going on around her. She called it rhythmic prayer. She explained to Maisie Ward in a letter,

> The idea that I have is that we are really part, as it were, of a vast rhythm, and that when we become more recollected we become more and more conscious of it. It cuts two ways. We can, I think, cultivate recollection by deliberately saying rhythms or poetry; and when we do this, those thoughts expressed within us rhythmically are heard by our minds in everything round us, even in the traffic in the street.[2]

Caryll deliberately wrote rhythms and sent them to people she knew to start some recollection in their souls. She used descriptions of ordinary, everyday happenings, inserting into them truths which she wanted to be woven right into people's being. Caryll realized that the rhythm not only had to be heard in the mind, it needed to be seen. So her images were often pictures, carved not in wood, but in words. She would deliberately put a single word on a line to make it stand out. She compared the structure of her rhythms to the different note values, chords, pauses, rests and counterpoint of musical scores. She sensed that through rhythms a plan for contemplation could be spread in the world.

Sheed & Ward published a collection of Caryll's rhythms in 1945 entitled *The Flowering Tree*. In an introductory note she points out:

> These rhythms are not intended to be poems in a new form, but simply thoughts falling naturally into the beat of the rhythm which is all round us and which becomes both audible and visible in the seasons of the year, the procession of day and night, and the liturgical cycle. They are arranged so that the rhythm and stress will be easily seen as well as thought, by people who are unused to reading verse. The theme which recurs in them is the flowering of Christ in [us].

Caryll understood prayer in a much wider context than "saying words." Through the repetition of rhythmic prayer throughout the day, we would come to realize that the very cycles of our lives are prayers: it is a prayer to rise in the morning, it is a prayer to work, it is a prayer to eat, it is a prayer to sleep.

Caryll illustrated the beauty of the habit of prayer with the story of a personal experience. She was conversing with a Jewish man who was building a sandbag wall when she accidentally dropped her crucifix. He insisted on undoing his wall to retrieve it. He stood looking at it, noting that he had never learned anything about Christ. Then he recalled that his mother had taught him a prayer that all Jewish mothers have taught their little sons to say as they are falling asleep at night from as far back as anyone can remember.

"What was it?" Caryll asked.

"Well, Miss, it went like this: 'Father, into Thy hands I commend my spirit.'"[3]

This kind of trust is at the heart of prayer. Caryll compares it to a cat lying by the fire in a state of complete abandonment. She says that even during times of peace we are too tense. It is a good plan to lie on the floor, sofa or bed and let ourselves go. However, all the elaborate techniques in the world do not relieve us of tension, she noted. Our bodies are not tense due to outside factors, but because the soul, which never for a moment ceases to act on the body, is tense. She proposed that those who suffer from anxiety do so because of an exaggerated sense of responsibility, a continual feeling of guilt, or attributing too much importance to their own work and not nearly enough to God's love and God's will. She suggested that a good exercise for such people would be to kneel down night after night and say one brief, simple and true prayer, "Dear God, my name is mud!"[4]

To pray always means to live in the presence of God at all times, to relax in the lap of God like the cat lying by the fire. It also means to live in the present moment, taking no thought of tomorrow. We are to look for God's gift in the moment, trusting in God's providence, knowing that even our sorrows are for our own good. Caryll proposes that we stop from time to time during a busy day to make a mental picture of two huge giving hands, God's hands, and to think, *"At this moment, God is handing me all I have."* Then she suggested that we mention everything that comes to mind. This is the opposite of the common tendency to focus on what we have not received which leads to bitterness, resentment, fear and despair. One of Caryll's rhythms states,

> My thoughts were like wild birds
> beating the bars of the cage
> for empty skies....
> Their voices went on and on in my head,
> monotonous waves wearing my mind away.
> (Rock is worn by the waves to sand.)
> I wanted to shut my mind,
> that my thoughts might
> close
> on my own peace; I wanted to close
> the peace of my love in my heart,
> like dew in a dark rose.[5]

Maisie Ward quotes a letter in which Caryll articulates her understanding of the experience of prayer: "Prayer *should* be a deep inner rest, something which calms you and increases your *trust* (the more it *does* increase your trust, the more it gives you inner peace and rest.)"[6]

Besides rhythmic prayer and relaxation, Caryll suggested that we change our attitude toward suffering. We must not, like the parents of the Buddha, try to keep the fact that there is suffering in the world from our children. Rather, we should teach them to suffer well. Caryll believed that the redemptive power of human suffering is a sharing in the passion and death of Christ. She was not so silly as to believe we would see results. She wrote,

> If my tooth aches and I take it well and offer it in
> love to God, I shall not see a slum dwelling dwindle

and flicker out like a spent candle and in its place an ideal home sprout up like a flower bursting from the bud. But the result happens—more grace, more courage, more hope on earth.[7]

Just as bitter, gloomy people can make hell on earth for those they meet, so those who suffer well bring joy and lighten the burdens of others. A grateful attitude is an essential element in life, she continues

> We shall desire to be grateful, to respond for every good thing, every flower or star, every moment spent happily, we shall want to thank someone, we shall want to be conscious of the presence of One Whom we can love without measure, in Whom we can delight without fear of loss, in Whom ultimately our grief will be lost as a flame is lost in the light of the sun.[8]

Exercise 11.1 Finding the Divine Presence in All Things

Materials needed: *Sets of chairs facing each other.*
Approximate time: *Thirty minutes.*
Script for Guide: Caryll found the presence of God in the rhythms of nature and the cycles of human life. More often than not, we become aware of the fact that the Divine Being is with us only in retrospect. It is by remembering those times when God did break into our lives that we become able to recognize the presence of the Divine in the present moment.

We are going to take some time now to evoke memories of God in our lives. Wander around the room until you find a partner and then sit down facing each other.

Move into inner stillness and close your eyes gently. In this quiet place, recall a time in your life when you felt the presence of God in a very special way. It may have been an experience connected with nature: watching the sun rise or set, sitting on the edge of a lake gazing into the water, or standing on a mountaintop surveying the beauty of the earth in all directions. It may have been a special moment in your life such as giving birth to a child or creating a work of art. It may have been a time of great suffering and pain. Move back into the atmosphere and emotional tone of that place and time and savor it for a few minutes. When you and your partner are both ready, share your memories with each other.

Group process: *After about fifteen minutes, or whenever you are aware that people have begun chatting rather than speaking and listening to each other's experiences, call the entire group together and invite them to state what kinds of experiences they noticed evoke a sense of God's presence. It is hoped that you will discover that there were times when they were totally present in the here and now, neither looking backward nor forward in time.*

For those working alone: *Move into inner stillness and close your eyes gently. In this quiet place, recall a time in your life when you felt the presence of God in a very special way. It may have been an experience connected with nature: watching the sun rise or set, sitting on the edge of a lake gazing into the water, or standing on a mountaintop surveying the beauty of the earth in all directions. It may have been a special moment in your life such as giving birth to a child or creating a work of art. It may have been a time of great suffering*

and pain. Move back into the atmosphere and emo-
tional tone of that place and time and savor it for a few
minutes. When you are ready, record what comes to
you in your journal.

Exercise 11.2 Meditation

Materials needed: *Journal paper and pen or pencil.*
Approximate time: *Thirty minutes.*
Script for Guide: St. Ignatius of Loyola (1491–1556)
suggested a method of prayer that exists in many traditions. Basically it involves the repetition of one word over
and over in the same tempo as the breath. This word is to
be considered as long as meanings, comparison, relish and
consolations come to the person praying. This method of
St. Ignatius differs from the simple repetition of a word
without thinking about it that is common in many traditions. He also suggests that whatever prayer position a
person chooses, the eyes are to be kept closed or to remain
fixed on one point. They are not allowed to wander. This
results in a greater ability to concentrate.

Now, finding a comfortable position, but not so comfortable that you fall asleep, close your eyelids gently. If
you prefer to keep your eyes open, focus upon a single
point in the room. Choose a single word or a favorite
prayer upon which you plan to meditate. It might be the
Our Father, Psalm 23, the Prayer of St. Francis, or a single word such as Father, Mother, Jesus, love, life or one.
(Pause)

Breathe in and out, allowing your breath to find its
own pace. *(Pause)* When you are ready, begin to say the
word under your breath, first as you breathe in, then as

you breathe out. Images, thoughts, memories, feelings and bodily sensations will arise spontaneously as you do this. Allow them to flow freely, continuing to say the word in time with your breath. Whenever you become aware of the fact that you have drifted away from this practice, begin again. Continue to say one word until you feel ready to move on to another. I will give you ten minutes to continue this practice now.

(Many find it helpful to use a chime or a Tibetan bowl to begin and end a period of meditation.)

Now, take ten more minutes to record what came to you as you meditated upon a single word at a time. What inner experiences did you have? What images, thoughts, memories, feelings, or body sensations were evoked? Did you feel anxious or bored?

Group process: *Share in the large group answers to these questions: What are your experiences saying to you? Do you see any value in this practice?*

For those working alone: *Choose a favorite scripture passage or a holy word. Practice repeating it according to the tempo of your breath. Ponder the meaning of the word or words as you repeat them. Do this for at least ten minutes. Then record in your journal your experience. Was focusing on the word or phrase easy or difficult? Did you find yourself drifting off? What thoughts came to you as you said the word or phrase? What is your experience saying to you? Do you see any value in this practice?*

Exercise 11.3 Rhythmic Prayer

Materials needed: *Handout of verses for prayer.*
Approximate time: *Thirty to forty-five minutes.*

Script for Guide: Another form of prayer that St. Ignatius taught was the repetition of words according to a rhythm or a beat. He called this *orar por compás*. The beat is that of the tempo of the breath. While saying each word, we are to reflect upon its meaning and at the same time keep in mind the Divine Person to whom the prayer is being addressed. The Book of Psalms is an excellent source for this type of prayer. The psalms express every human emotion from elation to despair and, like the lyrics of a song, their verses are rhythmic in nature.

The Jesus Prayer of the Russian pilgrim is another possibility. In English this prayer is "Jesus Christ, Son of God, have mercy on me." It goes as far back in history as the Greek fathers of the fifth century. By the fourteenth century it was widespread. St. Ignatius and his companions certainly knew about it. The constant repetition of a phrase connects us with that which transcends us. We move into a state of consciousness not governed by the ego, the will or the analytic intellect. This state enables us to feel a deep inner connection to that which lies beyond our individual lives while at the same time supporting and sustaining us.[9]

Caryll believed that the effect of rhythmic prayer is the quieting and easing of the heart that leads to an intense consciousness of God acting in us. It makes each moment so saturated with God that, as naturally as the flower opens to the light, we shall praise God merely by being what we were created to be.[10]

In J. D. Salinger's novel *Franny and Zooey*, an American schoolgirl who is looking desperately for some way to maintain her sanity decides to use the Russian pilgrim's techniques. Her efforts, however, end in disaster.

She passes out. Any attempt to adopt a spiritual practice that is not rooted in the context of our life nor done with adequate preparation results in the release of unharnessed energy that leads to an imbalance of mind, heart and soul. This imbalance may appear as ego inflation, depression or psychosis.

It is essential, therefore, that we walk our spiritual path with others, and not alone. A good spiritual companion or community helps us to contain the spiritual energy that meditation awakens in us.

Choose one of the following verses *(hand out sheet),* a vocal prayer that has meaning for you or any other group of words that you cherish, such as a line of poetry. You may also create your own verse or mantra. Then repeat the words according to the rhythm of your breath as St. Ignatius proposed. Continue to do this for at least fifteen minutes. I will keep time for you. Record your experience afterward, and then take time to share your experience in small groups (or pairs). *(Quotations may be copied and distributed.)*

> Have mercy on me, O God. (Ps 51:3)
> May the words of my mouth and the meditations
>   of my heart
> find favor in your sight, O Lord. (Ps 19:15)
> You anoint my head with oil; my cup is
>   overflowing (Ps 23:5)
> As the deer longs for flowing streams,
> my soul longs for you, O God. (Ps 42:2)
> Come, God's glory, burning in me.
>   (Caryll Houselander)

Exercise 11.4 Creating Your Own Rhythm

Materials needed: *Paper and pen, rhythm sticks, drums or anything that can be used to keep a beat, even slapping our hands on our knees. An audiocassette with a heartbeat such as* Environments 9/ Heartbeat *(New York: Syntonic Research, Inc., 1989) or drumming such as* Sacred Earth Drums *(Topanga, Calif.: Sequoia Records, 1994).*

Approximate time: *One hour.*

Script for Guide: Caryll realized that she couldn't simply dismiss her environment, all the interruptions or distractions that the day brings. So she wove her distractions right into her rhythms. They are filled with homely images of everyday life:

- the little boy on the bus standing to give his seat to a lady,
- the smell of lemon and soap and linen in the convent school,
- the monotony of things that link the years of a life,
- the faded flowers in a jam pot on a teacher's desk.

She included the truths she wanted to be woven right into a person's being with these images. For example,

- God abides in each of us.
- We are all called to be Christ in the world today.
- God's grace works secretly in us like yeast.
- God is not an old man in the clouds, but the seed of life in our soul.

120

- Our fears are not something to push out of sight like madmen behind bars.
- Dying and flowering are one thing.
- We are born out of another's pain and die in our own.

Now we are going to take the daily distractions of our own lives and weave our own truths with them by creating our own rhythms for ourselves and for the benefit of others.

(Play tape in the background.) (Guide beats drum to heartbeat.)

Poetry is the earliest form of language, going back to the first inarticulate cries of emotion. It is the language of the soul, of the heart, of the earliest mysteries of the world.[11] Its rhythms return us to the first sound we heard in the womb, the beating of our mother's heart. Creating our own rhythms returns us to the earliest pulsations of life and to our own creative impulses.

Take a pair of sticks, a drum, two spoons or anything else with which you can beat a rhythm. For a few minutes, we are going to beat our instruments to the sound of a heartbeat. As we enter into the rhythm, listen to the clicking of the sticks and to the booming of the drums:

- drums of the ancient Israelites celebrating the crossing of the Red Sea and deliverance from slavery,
- drums of the Native Americans connecting them to ancient wisdom and guiding the medicine man on his healing journey,
- drums of the jazz musicians in the heart of New Orleans,
- drums of rock 'n' roll bands,

- drums of soldiers going to battle,
- drums leading dead presidents to their graves,
- drums beating to the rhythms of the human heart,
- sacred sound beating to the rhythms of life—patterns moving through time beginning with the Big Bang,
- rhythms at the heart of the mystery of creation,
- rhythms of life.

(After five or ten minutes of drumming:)
Now stop your beating. Take a pen and a piece of paper and record and draw the images and memories, the thoughts and perceptions that came to you as you listened to the rhythms. I will give you about fifteen minutes to write and draw. *(Pause)*

Caryll Houselander used images and events of everyday life to create her rhythms. Now it's your turn. Take the images that came to you during the drumming or from other ordinary everyday experiences you have had and create your own rhythm. Use a minimum of words. Be vivid in your descriptions. Pay attention to the beat of the syllables. Say each line under your breath to feel its rhythm. Make sure it flows easily and trips smoothly over the tongue. Rewrite choppy and staccato phrases (unless they symbolize the nerve-wracking experiences that set your teeth on edge). I will give you about thirty minutes. I will let you know when it is time to return to the large group.

Group process: *Open the floor for reading aloud when most people are ready; then close by processing their experience. You may ask questions such as, "How was this exercise for you?"*

For those working alone: *For the first exercise in this chapter, you might spend some time recalling the times in your life when you felt God's presence and writing about them in your journal. The other three exercises can also be done on your own. You may want to read the Script for Guide in Exercise 11.4 onto a tape cassette and listen to it while you beat a drum or use some other rhythm instrument. Remember to reflect upon and record your experiences.*

Prayer

Mary, Mother of God,
we are the poor soil
and the dry dust;
we are hard with a cold frost.
Be warmth to the world;
be the thaw,
warm on the cold frost;
be the thaw that melts,
that the tender shoot of Christ,
piercing the hard heart,
flowers to a spring in us.
Be hands that are rocking the world
to a kind rhythm of love;
that the incoherence of war
and the chaos of our unrest
be soothed to a lullaby;
and the round and sorrowful world,
in your hands,
the cradle of God.[12]

Chapter 12:
Dry Wood and Shadows

It seems a law of fallen nature that life must always come to its being through darkness, and this makes us even more aware of its beauty. Dawn is lovelier because it comes after night, spring because it follows the winter.[1]

Caryll lived a mere nine years after the end of the Second World War. She had given up smoking and continued to eat very little. Her uncanny insight into human behavior and her books led to a merciless onrush of people in her life. She was besieged with requests to see her. Like so many who are in the middle of life, she had to devote more and more of her time and energy into caring for her aging parents and an elderly aunt. She wrote to a friend who had complained about how little time Caryll spent with her,

> My father is eighty, my mother seventy-five, and they live in the opposite ends of London. Each has to be visited at least once a week. Then I have an invalid aunt in Brighton, who would like a weekly visit but has to have a two-weekly one or less; there are several neurotic invalids who can't leave their homes, and several people in the

mental hospital, also requiring regular and frequent visits. My dinner when alone here only
takes about 15 minutes to cook and eat! Also I
continue to work while eating it.[2]

It would be interesting to know how her friend
responded when told a raft of people were more important than she was. Caryll's whole life might be summed
up as a total giving to others. Her experience of poverty
was having no time for herself: no time for solitude, no
time to think, no time to enjoy the pleasure of listening
to beautiful music, looking at the beauty of nature or
just curling up with a good book. She was a person
whose ears were continually filled with the troubles of
others, whose eyes saw the sorrow in the faces of others,
and whose hands touched others to heal, to comfort
and to bless. She was accessible to all who needed her,
but not always available to those whose friendship nurtured her. Once Caryll found refuge in her own illness,
spending an entire month in bed with pneumonia. She
enjoyed the solitude and the time it afforded to write a
book. As soon as she was better, Iris became ill and
Caryll had to nurse her. Then both of Caryll's parents
became gravely ill. Her father, then eighty-three, recovered but remained in precarious condition. Her mother,
on the other hand, stricken with cancer and tuberculosis, finally had to be moved into St. George's Hospital,
where Caryll and her sister Ruth shared day and night
vigils. Caryll left once a day to take a bath and rest one
or two hours in the morning. She had never seen anyone
suffer the way her mother did. Although her mother
had not received the sacraments in years, she confessed
her sins to a priest, received holy communion and was

anointed. From that moment on, her mother was peaceful and happy and died in that state. Caryll felt her mother's death deeply and suffered at the thought that she had not been a good daughter. "Something of oneself dies with one's mother," she said.[3] One month after her mother's death, Caryll and Iris spent Christmas at Chartres. Caryll came home with influenza. Then Iris came down with it and developed pleurisy. Nursing her became a full-time job for Caryll. Sometime during this period, Caryll suspected she had cancer. She was afraid to go to the doctor and find out because it might upset Iris. Her friend Rosamond pointed out how much more upsetting it would be if Caryll delayed too long. The cancer was on her left breast in precisely the same location as her mother's had been. Caryll wondered if this were "Gert's" revenge.

In April Caryll had surgery. She wrote to Iris from the public ward in the hospital that it was not for her to say "I must live" or "I must die" or to resist the humiliations and fears of the occasion. She would simply say with Christ "Into thy hands."[4]

The act of surrendering her diseased body and shivering soul to infinite Love was not as difficult for her as letting go of all those she loved, especially those whom she presumed were dependent upon her love. Caryll was released six weeks after her operation. She was not ready to die. In fact she realized that she had never allowed herself to truly enjoy life, so she was determined to spend what days remained rejoicing in the sheer loveliness of the world, the people in it, and even food, drink and spending money. In addition to writing a biography of her childhood, Caryll continued to carve works of art from wood and took great pleasure in caring for Iris' granddaughter, Clare.

As spring turned to summer in 1954, Caryll's health began to decline, even though her doctor told her she need not return for a check-up until the fall. Perhaps he knew there was nothing he could do for her. In that era, doctors had difficulty telling their patients that they were going to die. He told her that the symptoms she felt were not from cancer. She came home greatly relieved. When Iris visited the doctor a few weeks later, she insisted that he tell her the truth. He told her that Caryll did not have many months to live. She died on October 12, 1954, just a few weeks before her fifty-third birthday. Typically thinking not of her own suffering, but of another's, her last words to Iris were, "You must be very tired." Caryll wrote of the aging process and death in *The Risen Christ*:

> Sickness, old age, death, these must come; and when they come it seems that our service is ended. There is exhaustion which makes it first an effort, then an impossibility, to lift the hand up to make the sign of the cross; no more liturgical acts in daily life, gestures and symbols that worship God and give Christ's love. Everything falls away from us, even memories—even the weariness of Self. This is the breaking of the bread, the supreme moment in the prayer of the body, the end of the liturgy of our mortal lives, when we are broken for and in the communion of Christ's love to the whole world.
>
> But it is not the end of the prayer of the body. To that there is no end. Our dust pays homage to

127

God, until the endless morning of resurrection wakens our body, glorified.[5]

Her spirit lives on to inspire and encourage generation after generation of "seekers."

Exercise 12.1 Death and New Life

Materials needed: *"Resurrection" and "In Paradiso" from* Music to Disappear In *(San Francisco: Hearts of Space, 1988). "Lord of the Dance" by Sydney Carter (1963) for a final celebratory dance.*

Approximate time: *One hour.*

Script for Guide: People who are dying may see their entire lives flash before their eyes. Whatever the experience, no one who has come back from a near-death experience is known to have decided to spend more time working. Most return convinced that they are still on earth for a reason, and usually that is to tell everyone that love is the only thing that matters.

A meditation that has helped thousands of people to discover their true purpose in life is to imagine looking back at life from one's deathbed. We are going to do that now. So wander around the room until you find a partner, preferably someone you do not know too well, and when you have done so find a place to be together. Decide who is going to be the first one to imagine himself or herself dying. That person will lie on the floor while the other sits at his or her side.

You, who are dying, imagine yourself in bed surrounded by loved ones. Breathing has become difficult for you. You feel as if part of you is here and part of you is moving on to another place. You feel someone's hand holding yours gently. I will propose a series of questions. Your partner will repeat them. Speak your answers to that person who is standing in high witness to your living and to your dying. *(Allow adequate time between questions for the person to reflect and answer.)*

- What has made your life worth living?
- Do you have any regrets?
- What message do you want to leave for your family and friends?
- What do you fear?
- To what or whom do you find it most difficult to say good-bye?
- What has been most important to you in life, and what is most important in life to you now?
- Looking back over your life, is there anything you would have liked to have done differently?
- What are your hopes?

Now, held in your partner's arms, take three deep breaths, let go and die.

(While the music continues, read:)

Everywhere new fire is kindled and cast upon the earth. It is Christ dawning, Christ flowering in us now. We are made new, burning with the fire of his love. The seed dies. The wood of the cross blossoms with white flowers. Rise with new life now as you hear Christ announce to you, "See, I make all things new!"

Help your partner to rise and rejoice in this new life in Christ together. *(Pause)*

Next, the one who has been standing in high witness to a dying partner is to find a comfortable place to lie on the floor and I will repeat the same questions. The ones who have just risen to new life are to listen in high witness to their partners.

(After the second person has finished, invite all into an open space where all can dance their new life in Christ.)

Group process: *Spend a few minutes reflecting individually on the following questions and then share them with another person, in small groups or in the total group. What did you discover in this exercise? Is there anything about your life that you are going to change as a result? What?*

For those working alone: *Imagine yourself on your deathbed and answer the questions in the Script for Guide. When you are ready, reflect upon the questions under the Group Process above and record them in your journal.*

Exercise 12.2 Being Christ in the World Today

Materials needed: *A room cleared of chairs large enough for the entire group to form a circle.*

Approximate time: *Forty-five minutes.*

Script for Guide: Caryll assured us that we shall not be parted from those whom we love on earth. They will be hidden from us for a time however, a time that will pass swiftly. Then we shall be reunited with everyone we loved here forever, with no more fear of loss and with no shadow at all cast upon our human love. We have nothing to fear.[6]

We have nothing to fear from living, either. We know why we were born and what we are called to become.

When we shrink from our purpose in life, we live in confusion and turmoil. When we finally say yes to God's call, however timidly, our hearts are filled with peace and courage. This is the window of opportunity and challenge for each of us—to take the next step. What is yours?

Find a partner and share with each other what you have discovered your next steps are, especially the ways you may feel that you are being called to be Christ in the world today. They may be baby steps or giant leaps. The only thing that matters is that you take them. Once each of you has spoken, find some way to ritualize your next steps in gesture and in word. Each one of you can state your intention, taking turns. Speak your intention beginning with: "This is the way in which I feel I am to be Christ in the world today." Those who are listening and standing in the place of high witness are invited to bless and confirm what their partners have said. Address your partners by saying their name and then, "I confirm and bless___." See Christ in each other and be Christ for each other. *(Ten minutes)* When you are ready, help to form a circle where we will celebrate together our entry into the world as other Christs.

Group process: *Call the group together when you become aware of the celebration coming to a close. Sit on the floor or on chairs and share your experiences in the large group. What did you discover about each other? What are some of the "next steps" you need to take? How are you feeling about this experience right now?*

For those working alone: *You have arrived at an open moment in your life, that space between what has been* *and what will be. Record in your journal where you have been and what you feel strongly is the next step you need to take in your life. You may want to express this in the form of a poem, a prayer or a blessing.*

Prayer

Be born in us,
Incarnate Love.
Take our flesh and blood,
and give us Your humanity;
take our eyes, and give us Your vision;
take our minds,
and give us Your pure thought;
take our feet and set them in Your path;
take our hands
and fold them in Your prayer;
take our hearts
and give them Your will to love.[7]

Notes

Introduction

1. Caryll Houselander, *The Reed of God* (New York: Sheed & Ward, 1944), 80.

2. Caryll Houselander, *Guilt* (New York: Sheed & Ward, 1951), 88.

3. Ira Progoff, *Depth Psychology and Modern Man* (New York: McGraw-Hill Book Company, 1959), 249.

4. Michael Downey, ed., *The New Dictionary of Catholic Spirituality* (Collegeville, Minn.: The Liturgical Press, 1993), 681.

5. Jean Houston, *Godseed: The Journey of Christ* (Wheaton, Ill.: Quest Books, 1992).

6. Houselander, *The Reed of God,* 118.

7. Jean Houston, *The Search for the Beloved* (Los Angeles: Jeremy P. Tarcher, Inc., 1987), 104–113.

8. Maisie Ward, *Caryll Houselander That Divine Eccentric* (New York: Sheed & Ward, 1962), 161–162.

9. Caryll Houselander, "The Rosary," in *The Flowering Tree* (New York: Sheed & Ward, 1945), 77.

Chapter 1: Beginnings

1. Maisie Ward, *Caryll Houselander, That Divine Eccentric* (New York: Sheed & Ward, 1962), 315.

2. Caryll Houselander, "The Young Man," *The Flowering Tree* (New York: Sheed & Ward, 1945), 14.

3. Houselander, *The Reed of God* (New York: Sheed & Ward, 1944), 38–39.

4. Maisie Ward, *The Splendor of the Rosary with Prayers by Caryll Houselander* (New York: Sheed & Ward, 1945), 93.

Chapter 2: Sacred Wounding

1. Caryll Houselander, "The Parish First Communions," *The Flowering Tree*, 31.

2. Caryll Houselander, *A Rocking-Horse Catholic*, 36.

3. Houselander, *A Rocking-Horse Catholic*, 46.

4. Houselander, *A Rocking-Horse Catholic*, 54.

5. Caryll Houselander, *Guilt* (New York: Sheed & Ward, 1951), 77, 87.

6. This exercise is based upon material in "Chapter Ten: The Sacred Wound" of Jean Houston's *The Search for the Beloved* (Los Angeles: Jeremy P. Tarcher, Inc., 1987), 104–121.

Chapter 3: The Betrayal of Trust

1. A rhythm written by Caryll Houselander quoted in Maisie Ward, *Caryll Houselander, That Divine Eccentric*, 24.

2. Caryll Houselander, *A Rocking-Horse Catholic*, 59–60.

3. Maisie Ward, ed. "Letter to Christine Spender," in *The Letters of Caryll Houselander* (New York: Sheed & Ward, 1965), 111.

4. This exercise is based upon material in "Chapter Ten: The Sacred Wound" of Jean Houston's *The Search for the Beloved* (Los Angeles: Jeremy P. Tarcher, Inc., 1987), 104–121.

5. Ward, ed. "Letter to a Young Friend Who Married and Settled Abroad," in *The Letters of Caryll Houselander*, 119.

Chapter 4: Smoky

1. Caryll Houselander, *A Rocking-Horse Catholic*, 24.

2. Maisie Ward, *Caryll Houselander, That Divine Eccentric*, 93.

3. Houselander, *A Rocking-Horse Catholic,* 23.
4. Caryll Houselander, *Guilt,* 172–173.
5. I am indebted to Leslie Ayvazian, Remi Barclay Bosseau, Olympia Dukakis, and their "Voices of Earth" workshop for the concept of this exercise.
6. Caryll Houselander, "Mothers of the Unseen Christ," *Lift Up Your Hearts* (New York: Arena Lettres, 1979), 44–45.

Chapter 5: The Seeking
1. Caryll Houselander, *The Reed of God,* 108
2. Caryll Houselander, *A Rocking-Horse Catholic,* 129–130.
3. Maisie Ward, *Caryll Houselander, That Divine Eccentric,* 76.
4. Houselander, *The Reed of God,* 19.
5. Maisie Ward, *The Splendor of the Rosary with Prayers by Caryll Houselander* (New York: Sheed & Ward, 1945), 65.

Chapter 6: Visions
1. Caryll Houselander, *The Risen Christ* (New York: Sheed & Ward, 1958), 53.
2. Caryll Houselander, *A Rocking-Horse Catholic,* 73–74.
3. Caryll Houselander, "Advent," in *Lift Up Your Hearts,* 53.
4. Caryll Houselander, *The Way of the Cross* (New York: Sheed & Ward, 1955), 71–73.

Chapter 7: Coming Home
1. Caryll Houselander, *A Rocking-Horse Catholic,* 140.
2. Maisie Ward, *Caryll Houselander, That Divine Eccentric,* 108.
3. Ward, *Caryll Houselander, That Divine Eccentric,* 109.

4. Ward, *Caryll Houselander, That Divine Eccentric,* 89.

5. Ward, *Caryll Houselander, That Divine Eccentric,* 114–115.

6. Caryll Houselander, *The Way of the Cross,* 173.

Chapter 8: Sprats

1. Caryll Houselander, *The Reed of God,* 148.

2. Maisie Ward, *Caryll Houselander, That Divine Eccentric,* 128.

3. For a more complete description of the social artist, see Jean Houston's *A Mythic Life: Learning to Live Our Greater Story* (New York: HarperSanFrancisco, 1996), 298–304.

4. Caryll Houselander, *The Way of the Cross,* 61.

Chapter 9: War and the Passion of Christ

1. Caryll Houselander, *The Reed of God,* 70.

2. Maisie Ward, *Caryll Houselander, That Divine Eccentric,* 168.

3. Caryll Houselander, *Lift Up Your Hearts,* 81.

4. Ward, *Caryll Houselander, That Divine Eccentric,* 212.

5. Caryll Houselander, *The Way of the Cross* (New York: Sheed & Ward, 1955), 7–8.

6. Caryll Houselander, "The Adoration of the Cross (Westminster, 1942)," *The Flowering Tree,* 126.

7. Caryll Houselander, *This War Is the Passion,* 62.

8. Houselander, *The Way of the Cross,* 173.

Chapter 10: *Caryllinati*—Caryll's Wisdom School

1. Caryll Houselander, "Low Mass on Sunday," *The Flowering Tree,* 33.

2. Maisie Ward, *Caryll Houselander, That Divine Eccentric,* 175–176.

3. Maisie Ward, *The Letters of Caryll Houselander: Her Spiritual Legacy,* 103.

4. Ward, *Caryll Houselander, That Divine Eccentric,* 288.

5. Ward, *Caryll Houselander, That Divine Eccentric,* 262–263.

6. Ward, *Caryll Houselander, That Divine Eccentric,* 188.

7. Ward, *Caryll Houselander, That Divine Eccentric,* 189.

8. Caryll Houselander, *Guilt,* 168.

9. Caryll Houselander, *The Risen Christ,* 83.

10. Karl Menninger, M.D., *Whatever Became of Sin?* (New York: Hawthorn Books, Inc.), 1973.

11. Caryll Houselander, *The Way of the Cross,* 61.

Chapter 11: Rhythms

1. Caryll Houselander, *This War Is the Passion,* 83–84.

2. Caryll Houselander, "From a Letter of Maisie Ward," *The Flowering Tree,* i.

3. Houselander, *This War Is the Passion,* 87–88.

4. Houselander, *This War Is the Passion,* 104.

5. Houselander, excerpt from "Philip Speaks." *The Flowering Tree,* 58–59.

6. Maisie Ward, *Caryll Houselander, That Divine Eccentric,* 260.

7. Houselander, *This War Is the Passion,* 143.

8. Houselander, *This War Is the Passion,* 144.

9. Ira Progoff, *At a Journal Workshop* (Tarcher, 1992), 317.

10. Houselander, *This War Is the Passion,* 114.

11. This exercise is based partially on a process led by poet Judith Morley during a session on Emily Dickinson at Jean Houston's Mystery School in 1990. A transcript has been published in Jean Houston, *Public Like a Frog: Entering the Lives of Three Great Americans* (Wheaton, Ill.: Quest Books, 1993), 46.

12. Houselander, "The Reed," in *The Flowering Tree*, 67–68.

Chapter 12: Dry Wood and Shadows

1. Caryll Houselander, *Lift Up Your Hearts,* 77.

2. Maisie Ward, *Caryll Houselander, That Divine Eccentric,* 282–283.

3. Ward, *Caryll Houselander, That Divine Eccentric,* 290.

4. Ward, *Caryll Houselander, That Divine Eccentric,* 293.

5. Caryll Houselander, *The Risen Christ,* 73–74.

6. Caryll Houselander, *The Way of the Cross,* 170.

7. Caryll Houselander, "The Nativity," in Maisie Ward's *The Spendor of the Rosary* (New York: Sheed & Ward, 1945), 76.

Other Books in the Jung and Spirituality Series

CARL JUNG AND CHRISTIAN SPIRITUALITY
Edited by Robert L. Moore

JUNG AND CHRISTIANITY IN DIALOGUE
Faith, Feminism, and Hermeneutics
Edited by Robert L. Moore
and Daniel J. Meckel

LORD OF THE FOUR QUARTERS
The Mythology of Kingship
by John Weir Perry

THE WEB OF THE UNIVERSE
Jung, the "New Physics," and Human Spirituality
by John Hitchcock

SELF AND LIBERATION
The Jung-Buddhism Dialogue
Edited by Daniel J. Meckel
and Robert L. Moore

THE UNCONSCIOUS CHRISTIAN
Images of God in Dreams
by James A. Hall
Edited by Daniel J. Meckel

INDIVIDUATION AND THE ABSOLUTE
Hegel, Jung, and the Path Toward Wholeness
by Sean M. Kelly

JESUS' PARABLES
Finding Our God Within
by Robert Winterhalter with George W. Fisk

IN GOD'S SHADOW
The Collaboration of Victor White and C. G. Jung
by Ann Conrad Lammers

DANCING BETWEEN TWO WORLDS
Jung and the Native American Soul
by Fred R. Gustafson

JUNG AND SHAMANISM IN DIALOGUE
Retrieving the Soul/Retrieving the Sacred
by C. Michael Smith

RELIGION AND THE SPIRITUAL IN CARL JUNG
by Ann Belford Ulanov

JOURNEYS INTO EMPTINESS
by Robert Jingen Gunn